ARE WE NEARLY THERE YET?

Also by Sheila Bridge

The Art of Imperfect Parenting
The Art of Plate Spinning

First published in Great Britain in 1998

3 5 7 9 10 8 6 4 2

British Library Cataloguing in Publication Data
A record for this book is available from the British Library

ISBN 0 340 69463 7

Typeset by Palimpsest Book Production Limited,
Polmont, Stirlingshire
Printed and bound in Great Britain by
Clays Ltd, St Ives plc

Hodder and Stoughton
A division of Hodder Headline PLC
338 Euston Road
London NW1 3BH

Are We Nearly There Yet?

Sheila Bridge

Hodder & Stoughton
LONDON SYDNEY AUCKLAND

Monday, 1 January

It's New Year's Day and I'm not at my best. But then who is on the first day of a new year when you've had a late night celebrating the last day of the previous one? It's also a Monday. How inconsiderate.

It's a pity that merely turning over the first page of a fresh calendar fails to fire me with the enthusiasm necessary to carry through all my new year resolutions. As usual 'Lose weight and get fit' comes fairly near the top of the list, as I've over-indulged at Christmas. Then there's that book I received for Christmas: I must get round to reading it. And I've been so lax with my correspondence – perhaps my new writing paper will inspire me. The year is less than a day old and I am already compiling a mental list of 'must do', 'ought to', and 'have to' activities while simultaneously suffering a shortage of enthusiasm for any of them.

The children were up long before me this morning. Thankfully they beavered away quietly with their new colouring pens and creative kits. I wish I could have a share of their excitement; they abound with the stuff, even though it can be notoriously short-lived. They whizz round and make a lot of noise like some of the toys they had for Christmas, and it's a relief to everyone when the batteries finally run out. The chances are that their current passions for playing the violin and learning French will fizzle out just after I've paid for this term's tuition.

I shouldn't be so cynical; their liveliness inspires me. When they are keen on something they will read it, eat it or make friends with it ('it' being their library book, Gran's mushy peas or next door's cat respectively). In fact, if they are not thrilled by the task in hand, you may as well give up.

This morning I find myself wishing that I had such an uncomplicated approach to life. They can take this like-it-or-leave it approach because they are self-centred individuals with a diminished sense of responsibility. Wasn't it great being a kid? Maturity feels like a chore these days. Here am I, with a long list of grown-up resolutions and not an ounce of enthusiasm for any of them.

Wouldn't it be good simply to relish the pleasure found in each day the way my kids do? They are not driven by the tricky little phrases that complicate my adult life: 'I ought to' or 'I should'. They don't need to have a reason for doing something, and they are not much bothered by the end result either. They get uncomplicated pleasure out of simple activities. Before Christmas they spent a whole afternoon collecting all the acorns that had fallen from an oak tree in our garden. On the face of it, the only result of this futile exercise was a pile of 176 acorns laid to rest in a corner of the flowerbed, but you couldn't have measured the enjoyment they'd had from this meaningless task.

If I resolve to do anything this year, it should be to learn as much as I can from my kids. I should stop assessing my worth by my output, my achievements by the number of items I've ticked off on my list. After all, I don't value my children that way. I value them for their enthusiasm – for their efforts, not for their successes.

I remember playing a board game with my son Matthew when he was a lot smaller. He had two friends round to play, and they had all been keen at the suggestion of a game and greatly enjoyed throwing the dice. After a while I realised that that was all they were enjoying. None of them could reliably count further than four and they didn't have a single game plan between them. I was the person moving the counters and telling each child where he was going and why. At one point my superior adult self tapped me on the shoulder and told me that as I was, in fact, playing this game by myself, in a sort of four-part harmony, with four helpers to throw the dice, why didn't I simply put the board away and let them just throw the dice in turns? I rejected this grown-up common sense and played on. So what if they didn't have a game plan? They had enthusiasm.

So why is it that my energy level is at an all-time low this morning? Have I become a middle-aged cynic overnight, or am I just suffering from the excesses of the season? Neither. I think my supply of zest has been slowing, seeping away, over several months. I haven't felt the same ever since my sudden return to secondary teaching last October. After five years out of the classroom, going back has been a draining and exhausting experience.

And it's only a part-time post. How on earth do other mothers cope with full-time jobs? I suppose they give up other responsibilities. The difficulty with part-time work is that I think I can squeeze all the part-time bits of my life around my part-time job. Perhaps that's why I now feel my brain has gone out to lunch without me and I don't know where to begin getting organised. But get organised I must. Having bungled Christmas in several ways, the pressure to pull myself up by my own shoelaces is now overwhelming. Not surprisingly, in the midst of all this my spiritual life has also nosedived, and the routines that used to hold me together (prayer, Bible study) feel like just two more chores on the list.

I was mulling all this over last night as I sat in my bath feeling miserable (what a great way to spend New Year's Eve). When I pulled out the plug and felt the warm, soothing water draining away, I thought, *This is just what I feel like. All the comforting certainties of life have been drained away*. It was as if I had lived all my life in a warm bath of faith and suddenly someone had silently pulled the plug. All my confidence, assurance and competence appeared to have soaked away. It felt easy to believe that I was a waste of space, and none of things I used to feel so sure about consoled me.

Even though I could explain my state of mind, I didn't find the reasons for it consoling. You can feel very cold, naked and vulnerable sitting in an empty bath, whether it's an emotional bath or a real one. What I wanted was for someone to pick me up, rub me down and put me back on my feet. But God didn't seem to be on hand with the towel.

So how come my bath of faith had once been full anyway? Where had my warm feelings of faith, security and certainty come from? From the fact that I'd been brought up in a Christian home by people who never doubted God's active involvement with life? Or did it flow from the fact that I'd led a safe, relatively easy life in which nothing had really challenged my faith? Or did my full bath of faith rely on my previous disciplines of prayer, reading and Bible study?

Returning to work has wrecked these routines. Perhaps all I need to do is to take myself in hand and get back to reading: that weighty book I got for Christmas would be a good place to start. But, listen to me – here I am back to my lists again. I feel as if I'm trying to plug my faith leaks for myself. Trying to pull myself up spiritually by my own efforts. What's God's role in all this? Surely it's his job to keep the bath full?

This morning, following on from my bath-time meditation, I happened to pick up another book. It wasn't the weighty one on my list. It was a slim volume, lent to me by a friend, and it had big print. This helped enormously because it happened to be on church history, not usually a subject that inspires me.

I read a chapter about Martin Luther. The book came to life in my hands as I discovered that he had written all about what happens when our faith seems to drain away when it comes into conflict with our experience of life. He'd called this experience a 'vortex of faith', when the daily grind of life seems to suck away our awareness of God and the bigger picture. What he had to say was so reminiscent of my own plug-hole devotions that I couldn't put the book down without finding out his conclusions. He said that faith came from God – in other words, we cannot fill up the bath by ourselves. No amount of self-discipline or warm fellowship can be a substitute for the gift of faith from God. This comforted me hugely. I did not have to find faith, which I felt I no longer had, from somewhere in myself. I simply had to ask God for it. It was God's job to fill up the bath of faith and then to get me out of the bath and into action again.

Later on I did get round to the weighty tome I got for Christmas because spending New Year at Gran's has allowed me more kid-free moments than normal. When I opened it I read these words:

'The state of being dried up, of feeling one's natural abilities and qualities to be at an end, is good. God requires that we depend on him totally to clothe us with his life.' I take this as further encouragement that it is okay to feel spiritually cold, naked and vulnerable and that the only thing to do in this situation is to leave it up to God to get you out of the bath and dressed for action. Recognising that I feel this way and handing it over to God may actually be the first step to recovery. Well, a first step on the first day – it's a start.

Monday, 8 January

Monday again and I'm suffering from an identity crisis: last night I was the tooth fairy, this morning I am the schoolteacher, by teatime I will be Mummy again. In between, I will be either a housewife or possibly a writer. This is the usual extent of my repertoire.

The schoolteacher bit gives rise to two common nightmares: the one where you are trying to get out of the house on time and can't find anything you need, and the one where you arrive at work in your night-clothes.

Anyone living with a similar number of identities will understand the fear of finding oneself in the wrong clothing at the wrong time. This morning I am in schoolteacher mode: court shoes, smart skirt

'... she does not entirely approve'

and shirt. But this working wardrobe has created some problems for my perceptive daughter Emma. The leggings and long jumpers of plain old Mummy have gone, and she does not entirely approve.

As far as she is concerned, her mother's earlier career as a teacher is an unsubstantiated myth from that period of history that predates her birth. In Emma's eyes, teachers are supreme beings. She lives in awe of them and has often aspired to be one; therefore Mummy can't possibly be a teacher.

As usual, her inner confusion has resulted in outward disruption.

Despairing of her unreasonable behaviour, I related all this to my prayer partner last night and we prayed for patience, again. As we prayed I was suddenly able to see the situation from Emma's point of view: she simply did not know how to respond to this Mummy/teacher hybrid. When I had been just Mummy, the ground rules were understood: she could fight, lie, cheat, beat up her brother and still be loved (not that she did all of these things everyday, you understand). But now that I was a teacher at the big school, how should she behave? She is one of life's diligent little beings, but even she couldn't face the prospect of twenty-four-hour best behaviour. Hence the rebellion.

The result of this insight is that tonight, before I pick her up from school, I will quickly change my clothes at home and hide the set of books I have to mark.

Tuesday, 9 January

It worked! A simple change of clothing sent the message that I am still Mummy. It may take her a little longer to adjust to the fact that ordinary people like me, who forget things, burn dinners and watch *Gladiators*, can also be teachers, but I think it's a good lesson to learn.

Thursday, 11 January

Today I drained my resources of patience. All day my ears had been assaulted with demands for my attention. At school, it was 'Miss, Miss, Miss' (not a reflection of my marital status); at home it was 'Mum, Mum, Mum'. The needle hit zero just as my husband, David, walked in the door with his usual cheerful enquiry: 'What's for tea, dear?'

This was unfortunate . . . for him.

It was even more galling for me because I am currently leading a parenting course. This is the week we were meant to be practising 'listening and speaking respectfully'. I'd been doing really well up until teatime today. I'd become so polite I was even waiting for the man on the radio to finish his sentence before I turned him off. Now I'd blown it.

Friday, 12 January

Last night, as a penance, I read the homework for this week of our parenting course. It was all about 'accepting your child's negative feelings'. I resolved to try harder with this new assignment.

This morning Emma was meant to return to school after a few days off with a cold. I wanted her to take a purse of tissues slung over her shoulder in case she needed to blow her nose. Her feelings about this suggestion were (a) embarrassment – 'The other children will laugh at me' – and (b) fear – 'It might not be allowed.'

Did I listen to these negative feelings with receptive acceptance? No, I did not. *My* feelings were that *her* feelings were unco-operative and illogical. Privately, I was also feeling uncertain and guilty about sending a still sniffing child back to school, but I badly needed the personal space and she was more or less over the cold. Given that it was twenty to nine and we were almost out of the door when the dispute arose, the row that resulted from this clash of negative feelings was hardly surprising. All over some tissues. Can you believe it?

The upshot of it all was that I kept her off school for another day, ran around headless for half an hour arranging cover for my classes and eventually went back to the parenting manual to look up the section on 'Restoration after a Row'. I followed it to the letter.

Saturday, 13 January – the facts of life

Why is it that children have a tendency to ask those disarmingly huge questions about life, God and the universe at either the earliest possible moment in the day, just as you are blinking your way into bleary-eyed awareness of life, or at some particularly inconvenient moment, while you are in polite company with posh aunties or ploughing your weekly way round the supermarket?

I have a friend who has twice explained the facts of life to her daughter, both times in Toys 'Я' Us. For the life of me I can't think how the ambience of this particular chainstore should prompt such a question once, let alone twice. (Perhaps on the second occasion she just remembered how interesting the first visit was!)

While I stoutly defend the theory that any reasonable question deserves a reasonable answer, no matter how inconvenient the time or place, I have to admit that too many questions, too early in the day, leave me weary and irritated.

My own daughter's curiosity about life seemed to peak at the age of five. If anyone had analysed her conversation at that stage they would have found it 92 per cent proof in terms of questions. Put her in a new situation, and the question content of her conversation rose to a staggering 99 per cent (the remaining 1 per cent merely being statements leading up to questions – for example, 'I'm hungry. When will tea be ready?').

Now she is six and 'clever as clever'. (A. A. Milne was obviously well acquainted with a six-year-old.) Either she is no longer curious or she has written her mother off as an unreliable source of information. Either way, I get far fewer questions these days. Instead she likes me to think up really hard questions for her to answer.

This is how we came to be practising mental arithmetic at 7.30 this morning.

She is currently fascinated by numbers, but her fascination is somewhat limited by the fact that she cannot yet add up without the help of her fingers. She gets around this problem by giving the appearance that she is working out any given sum in her head while at the same time contorting herself into unnatural positions that allow her a sneaky view of her digits.

After a few minutes of 'What's three plus four?', 'Five plus two?', 'One plus six?' she tired of the easy-peasy stuff and decided to test me. Trying to think of the hardest sum imaginable, she came up with 'What's ninety-nine plus ninety-nine?'

She was very surprised when I gave her the answer. So was I. Given that I am numerically challenged, and that it was very early in the morning, 189 was a pretty near miss. The sweet, trusting child, who had no way of verifying my answer, stopped to look impressed for a moment. But not for long. With a gleam in her eye she came out with the next disarmingly huge question.

'What's infinity plus two?'

As her father is a doctor of physics, I guess I should have expected something like this. Some time ago, during a discussion about big numbers, she had asked her dad what was the biggest number. 'Infinity,' he had replied.

'Great,' was the enthusiastic response. 'Can we count to infinity before bedtime?'

Ever since then this concept has gripped her imagination. Pleased that her question had silenced me, she confided that Paul in her class would be able to write down *all* of the infinity number.

'Can he really?' I asked, wondering if some child prodigy lay dormant in Year Two of Paddox First School.

'Yes, I'm sure he can because, you see,' she explained patiently, 'his handwriting is very small.'

Matthew also has this canny knack of seeing life simply. As I was pedalling along on my bike one day he announced from the comfort of his rear seat, 'We don't put petrol in bikes, do we, Mummy?'

'No, Matthew, we don't.'

Before I could think of a simple way to explain the connection between his mother's breathless exhaustion and our propulsion along the street, he came up with this observation.

'There's no holes in bikes. There's only holes in

cars. So we only put petrol in cars.' He sounded very pleased with his conclusion. Never mind the internal workings of a combustion engine. Matthew only required a hole.

It was his powers of observation that led to the latest large question: where had he come from? The issue arose last night when we were in the bath together. We were not alone; his sister had joined us and one Jersey cow. The cow, thankfully, was small and plastic, the children were wet and giggly and I was tolerating this bath-share situation only on account of my green instincts.

'Mummy, you've got a fat tummy,' my daughter remarked.

Before I could protest or even pull it in, Matthew had colluded with his sister's opinion about my midriff, adding, 'It's 'cos we growed in there, isn't it?'

Grateful for a graceful way out, I readily agreed, although as Matthew is now at school this is a pathetic excuse. Still, at least his comment revealed his understanding of the simplest fact of life. I felt reassured that they seemed so contentedly matter-of-fact about the place where they'd 'growed'. It all seemed perfectly natural. Well, of course, it *is* natural. We know that, but try explaining it in simple terms to a small child and you'll find it sounds quite ridiculous.

'I grew in your tummy? Why not in your arm? What did I eat? Was Teddy there too?'

So how does a small child come to terms with the idea of growing in Mummy's tummy? Frankly, I have no idea, but I have learnt that terminology may be important. Ever since a certain careless conversation around the family teatable, I have been very careful to call all the parts of the anatomy by their proper names. We had been discussing who had grown in whose tummy. The children liked working out which of their parents had grown in which grandma and, for some odd reason, wanted reassurance that Daddy had not grown in Mummy's tummy. (They asked very casually, in a 'just checking' sort of way. Do I look that old? Do I mother him?)

Anyway, I could see Matthew was struggling with this concept of growing in tummies. His brow was furrowed in concentration and eventually he voiced his alarming confusion. 'Mummy,' he earnestly enquired, 'you didn't eat me, did you?'

The poor lad's eyes were round with horror, thinking that the only way he could have got into Mummy's tummy was the same way anything else got into it.

I hastily assured him that I had not eaten him, and the official line is now 'You grew in Mummy's womb.'

Time will tell if this has been a more helpful explanation. He has yet to enquire how he came to grow in this location. I'm waiting for the ultimately disarming question: 'Which "woom" did I grow in,

Mummy? Was it the front "woom" or the back "woom"?'

When the questions become wearisome I remind myself that I am not called to be all-wise and all-knowing. I am not an expert at everything. It's okay to say, 'I don't know. Let's find out,' and I know that whatever I do say, I will always be wrong.

I remember a conversation I had with Emma on holiday last year. We were watching the waves pound in on a seashore.

'Who turns the waves off?' she asked.

'No one does. The wind whips up the waves, and then the tides make them bigger too . . . I think.' Realising that I was on what was, for me, unsafe scientific territory, I faltered. David wasn't around to help, so I changed tack and took the question into a spiritual dimension. 'Of course, God can turn the waves off. Do you remember how Jesus stilled the storm for his disciples in the boat?'

Giving me a look that said, 'Yes, yes, I know all about God and that,' she called up the one singular fact from her store of experience that refuted all this waffle Mummy was giving her about wind and tides. 'There's a man to turn them off at the swimming pool.'

She had me cornered.

'Well, okay,' I had to admit. 'I don't know how they can be turned off but I know a man who can.'

Monday, 15 January

Over the weekend David and I fell in love. Not with each other, as it happens, although this would have been quite acceptable, even understandable, in the light of all the recent discussions about sex. We fell in love with a house.

We hadn't really meant to go house-hunting. We've known for at least a year that a move was inevitable, given the fact that our walls are not elastic, but we weren't seriously looking. I just happened to see a local house that seemed, on paper, to be ideal, so we made an appointment. Purely for the purposes of comparison, we plucked the details of another house, in another part of town, from a pile of possibilities and went to see that one as well.

We fell for the one further away. Further away from here, that is, and further from the children's school but closer to church.

It's hard to say how it happened. Falling in love is always rather hard to define. We walked into the hall and were impressed. We continued into the kitchen and went all soft inside. It reminded both of us of the kitchen in our first house. After that, well, love is blind. The fact that there was one bedroom fewer than we required seemed a trivial concern.

All week we've been held in the grip of that 'this is it' feeling, with only the occasional moment of doubt. Have we been duped by the lovely decor? Quite likely, given that we've always moved when it's been time to decorate. Perhaps we've been dazzled by the cherry-red Aga in the kitchen or the jacuzzi in the bathroom. Rather OTT for a semi, but we could cope.

Today we are going to talk to the bank, so it must be serious. Last night, as David pulled out his Bible as usual, I told him I'd hardly dared read mine for fear of using it as a crystal ball. When you are desperate for some guidance on a big decision, this is all too tempting. My reading for yesterday had been Jeremiah 29:5–11: 'Build houses and settle down . . . For I know the plans I have for you.' This seemed deliciously appropriate.

But I kept quiet about it until David disclosed that his text for the day was 'Sell all your possessions.' You have to understand David's prudent approach to finances to appreciate the amusement this gave us. The prospect of any large financial outlay causes David to suck in his breath sharply and shake his head doubtfully. Such wildly extravagant gestures of faith are not really his ballgame.

'Well, at the very least it's a directive to sell,' I suggested. He looked doubtful.

So, should we or shouldn't we? Will we or won't we?

Tuesday, 16 January

Our personal house-move decision was reflected last night at a specially convened church meeting.

It wasn't that we'd called the whole church together to discuss our domestic decision; we were meeting to consider the potential purchase of a property in our parish for the purposes of a church centre.

Our wise and beloved leader gave us the task of considering all the possibilities and practicalities of the proposal. I thought he was a genius to have chosen two such neutral and inoffensive words to describe the extremes of opinion that were, no doubt, represented in the room. 'Some people thrive on chances and choices,' he explained. 'Others feel far more at home with firm facts and figures.'

This wasn't news to me. In our marriage there is a 'possibility person', me, and a 'practicality person', David. The tension arising from having these two perspectives on life represented in one marriage has not always been creative.

'We could do this.'

'It'd cost too much.'

'We could go there.'

'It's too far away.'

'It might not be so bad.'

'It could be worse.'

You get the idea.

Over the years, however, I have come to appreciate David's practical nature. Yesterday, I combined him with a calculator and two sets of house details (our current residence and our prospective residence) and left him alone for five minutes. When I returned he had worked out the area in square metres for each room of both houses. Then he compared the two and came up with several statistical gems, the most memorable being the fact that Matthew's new room would be 89 per cent bigger than his present room, which makes it sound as if we presently store him in a cupboard!

Far from being inspired, David went all the way to the bank sighing, 'They'll never loan us that much.' I've learnt to ignore such doom-laden remarks.

Not only were they happy to loan us 'that much', they even threw in another year's discount for fun. David was overwhelmed. It's not fair: pessimists always get to be pleasantly surprised. So we've picked the house and arranged the finance. All we need now is a buyer for our current house.

I have to admit all this house-buying excitement has distracted me somewhat from my lack of spiritual buoyancy at the start of the year. But my bath of faith is slowly filling. Learning from the way I relate to the kids, I'm reminding myself that my heavenly Father doesn't need a reason to love me, and I don't need a result or a rigorous set of disciplines to impress him. I don't need to succeed or be organised for him to love to spend time with me. Just as I played a game with my son and his friends, God is engaging me in the game of life, like an infinitely wise parent playing Ludo with a three-year-old. If my lack of strategy infuriates him, he never lets on.

I realised that relying on Jeremiah 29:11 regarding the house move might be a bit of simplistic thinking on my part when I came across Jeremiah 22:13–14, which reads, 'Woe to him who . . . says, "I will build myself a great palace with spacious upper rooms."' Discerning divine directions is no easy task.

Tuesday, 23 January

Our home group from church met tonight in our house. Two weeks ago, when we last met, I came clean and shared with them the thoughts I'd had over New Year, the sense that someone had pulled the plug on my faith and confidence and I was left feeling very cold and naked in an empty bath. They had listened with understanding and sympathy and thankfully no one offered any sure-fire, instant spiritual solutions (Christians are often so prone to give black-and-white answers to rainbow questions). But I'm sure several of them went away and prayed for me, and I've appreciated their silent support. This morning in my reading I came across Isaiah 61:10: '. . . he has clothed me with garments of salvation and arrayed me in a robe of righteousness.' I read it several times and then I underlined it and then, for good measure, I committed it to memory with the help of actions. It sums up all that I learnt from Luther on New Year's Day: your faith, your security, your comfort are all down to God. It is God's responsibility to get us out of the bath and clothe us with faith, and he is doing that for me.

I did eventually get further on with the weighty book I got for Christmas, devotional readings by Oswald Chambers. The other day, in the midst of all the uncertainty regarding the possible house move, I read these words: 'As you journey with God, the only thing he intends to be clear is the way he deals with your soul.' It's a sad fact of my little life that God is still trying to wean me off my preoccupation with the petty (where I am going to live) and involve me with the important (deepening my understanding of his love for me).

I taught the verse in Isaiah to everyone at home group, complete with actions.

Thursday, 1 February

I guess a diary is the right place for embarrassing personal revelations, so here's one to be going on with: whenever David is away I go to sleep holding one of his hankies.

I probably had some justifiable excuse, like a cold, when this habit took hold, but now I have to confess it is just a reassuring ritual, a comforting token of his presence.

David is very attached to his handkerchiefs. He's never without one. His mother taught him that decent chaps always have their top button done up and carry a clean hanky every day. The first lesson was lost on him but not the second.

For David, it's a case of IN EMERGENCY, APPLY

'... he was six inches under by four o'clock'

HANKY. It covers children's grazed knees, extracts foreign objects from eyes and has been proffered for every emotional trauma I've ever been through.

There's been a heavy demand for his hankies this week. Unfortunately, David left last Saturday on a business trip, depriving us of at least seven hankies and his comforting presence. Within hours of his departure I had gone down with a stinker of a cold.

Then on Tuesday the guinea pig died. This was very inconsiderate of him; I'd just bought a new bale of hay and a barrel of food, a foolish investment to make in a geriatric guinea pig. We found him with his face and two front paws in his feeding bowl, so we reckon he died happy.

I'm a bit squeamish about stiff guinea pigs, so I wondered what I was going to do with the corpse. I needn't have worried, Matthew, who'll make a great pathologist one day, was fascinated and promptly picked it up.

Swallowing my instinctive 'don't touch' response, I saw my chance to avoid handling it myself. I instructed Matthew to 'hold on till I fetch some newspaper'. Once it was wrapped in several sheets of the local paper as a makeshift shroud, I felt I could cope.

From previous experience I have learnt that the children feel obliged to cry until a dead pet is decently buried, so we didn't hang about. He was six inches under by four o'clock, a mere twenty minutes after we found him. (I know six inches isn't much, but 'the earth stood hard as iron'. I did my best.)

Four o'clock on Wednesday brought a loss of a different kind. A phone call from the estate agents to say that 'our' house, the one we had fallen for, had been sold to someone else. Needless to say, there isn't a buyer in sight for ours.

Several soaked hankies later, I told the children. David won't hear about all this until he gets back on Saturday, which leaves me holding the hanky for two more nights. I think I'll make it . . . just.

The Psalmist had warlike images of God which comforted him ('my shield', 'my fortress'). As metaphors for God these do not always do a great deal for me. My own metaphors may not have quite the same ring to them but 'my pillow', 'my blanket', and 'my hanky' speak volumes to me.

Wednesday, 7 February – trying to learn contentment

It's a week now since the purchase of the house we wanted fell through. I have been trying to come to terms with the disappointment. Where I was going to live and when I was going to live there had become map references for the future, and now it feels as if someone had redrawn the map. I still feel a little lost.

I live with someone who seems permanently lost

in space and time. For Matthew the discovery that it was Wednesday today came as a complete surprise – for all he knew it was Friday or Monday. For the rest of us such landmarks have become vital, but when you can't tell the time and have only a vague idea of where you live, I don't suppose it matters much what day of the week it is. What does matter is to be content, and Matthew is the most content individual I know.

We have tried teaching him the days of the week, but as far as he is concerned there are only three days: 'school days', 'church days' and 'treat days'. 'Treat days' are Saturdays, when he gets to spend his pocket-money at the local shop. The other two are self-explanatory. There are too many school days in the average week for his liking, but he is usually content with his lot.

Regarding his location, we have spent a long time trying to teach him his address. 'Where do you live?' my husband drills him. He will happily rattle off the house number and street name but the town concept has him stumped. On one occasion, after a long pause and a lot of hard thinking, he eventually offered, 'Sainsbury's?'

Still, even if he doesn't know what day it is or where he lives, he is sure about several other matters. He has chosen a wife. 'Suzanna's going to marry me, Mummy,' he told me a few months ago, 'and so am I!' he added for good measure.

And, for a career, he's opted to be an 'air-driver'. It

took us a little while to work this one out, but having rejected the set of similar-sounding equivalents (hair drier, bus driver . . .) it suddenly came to us: a pilot, of course. How conveniently in tune with his father's aspirations!

I'm encouraging him to keep an open mind on these major life choices, but as life is such a steep learning curve when you are only four I suppose it helps to feel you've got a few things settled.

The other night he was sitting reading, and as I listened to the staccato delivery of a small child learning to read and watched him stab at each word with his fat little finger, I realised that you can learn a lot about contentment from living with a small person like Matthew.

Contentment is not being sure of all of the things we grown-ups expect to be sure about, such as the day of the week, or the name of our town, or even where will we be living in six months' time. Instead contentment is knowing that someone else knows these things. Contentment is trusting that there is a someone who will tell us what we need to know when we need to know it. For Matthew, that reliable someone is usually me.

'It's Monday, Matthew. Put your school clothes on.' 'It's Wednesday, Matthew. Take your library book.'

He's totally accepting of my advice. If I told him we were going to swim the Channel today, he'd probably get out his swimming trunks. I have so much to learn from such passive, unquestioning compliance. It makes a nice change, coming as it does after the onslaught of his older sibling's investigative approach to life.

My daughter takes nothing for granted. She is currently conducting an experiment to see if there are, in fact, 365 days in a year. She began on her birthday last year and has dedicated an entire notebook to her tally of days. On 20 July this year she will have her answer . . . shame it's a leap year!

My children represent two approaches to life: the laid-back, 'let's see what turns up' style of living, and the supervising, 'let's check this out' approach. It's when I come up against situations that I cannot control or check out that I need to learn contentment from someone like Matthew. I need to trust in the presence of someone who knows all that needs to be known.

Last week, as he sat dripping on the bench after his swimming lesson, Matthew looked up into his father's face and asked in all seriousness, 'Have you been to the moon, Daddy?'

'No, Matthew, I haven't.'

'I'd like to go to the moon. Is it far?'

'Well, yes,' David said, sitting back for a serious chat. 'It takes about four days in a rocket.'

Matthew turned over in his mind the possibilities of such a perilous journey. 'So, it's beyond the sky then? How do astronauts know where it is? Do they have to leave at night so they can see it?' (Visions of an astronaut type leaning out of his rocket window saying, 'There is it, men. Follow that moon.')

'Well, no, it's not quite like that, Matthew.' David was struggling. It isn't easy explaining space travel to someone for whom Grandma's house is the edge of the known universe.

Matthew's faith in his father's capacity to do anything and everything is very moving. Why shouldn't his dad have been to the moon?

Perhaps when I struggle with dreams or aspirations that seem so far beyond my reach that I feel like a child reaching for the moon, I should remind myself that I also have a someone who knows life's uncertainties. I too have a Father, but my Father has not only been to the moon; he put it there in the first place.

Wednesday, 14 February

This morning we were woken by the children who, much to our surprise, came into the room carrying a banner declaring, 'It's Valnetines Day!' This labour of love, complete with spelling error, had been all their own idea. They accompanied it with a song composed by Emma. Matthew delivered the song. Emma played the recorder. The reason for their enthusiasm became obvious in the words of the song:

It's Valentine's day,

It's Valentine's day,
A day for giving cards
And probably presents too!

The last line was delivered with meaningful grins in our direction. With Christmas a relatively recent memory, they obviously had hopeful expectations of the next festival. They had heard about it on *Blue Peter* and had even made the heart-shaped cardboard box just like the one on the programme. This they duly presented to us, filled with Rolos and Polos, some of which appeared to have been nibbled already.

It was wonderful. Such an unexpected and totally unprompted outpouring of love so early in the morning! We were overwhelmed. The children, however, were disappointed. When it became obvious that all that happened on Valentine's Day was the exchange of soppy cards between their parents, they stomped off downstairs, complaining loudly about the biased adult nature of the celebration.

We did share the sweets with them.

Friday, 23 February: half-term, health farms and high hopes

This week off school has been a boon. Today my sister-in-law and I opened our Christmas presents. Becky has a very high-stress job, so for Christmas David and I had given her a day at a health farm to help her unwind. My mother-in-law, knowing about our gift, had given me the same gift so that Becky and I could go together.

We've had a great day. We swam in the pool, sweated in the sauna, exercised in the gym, ate a healthy lunch in the restaurant and dozed in the chairs. We've been cosseted from head to foot, had our fingernails painted and covered ourselves with lotions and potions. I'd chosen some banana shower cream and avocado moisturiser, so I came home smelling like a fruit salad.

Appropriately, I'm reading the book of Esther. She spent six months in oil of myrrh and six months in cosmetics and perfumes. Six months in each department! A whole year at a health farm. I could take that kind of calling, Lord.

We made the most of our one day and I made the most of the whole week for some spiritual replenishment. I started by reading Proverbs, but then I decided that I'd like to read the whole Bible through again, so to spur me on I bought myself a new version. I have read the whole thing through before, so I do realise it'll take me longer than one half-term, but you have to start somewhere. David and I read it through by the same plan during the year before we were married. I'm sure I made it to Revelation only because reading it together gave the undertaking a competitive edge. I was not going to be the one who gave up. David's motives were purer no doubt.

That was over a decade ago, so a determination to repeat the exercise is long overdue. This time I've abandoned a plan; I am simply going to record on the inside front cover of my new cheap paperback version a list of the books I've read. When there are sixty-six books noted on the front cover I'll know I've made it.

There are several other spin-offs to buying a cheap Bible. It has the firm but floppy feel of an airport novel, those books you only read on holiday to veg out. This makes Bible reading feel like a self-indulgent pleasure. I've even started carrying it around the house with me and reading chunks of it whenever I get the time. If I get caught reading when I should be otherwise employed, it slots neatly down the back of the sofa.

The second spin-off is that the recycled paper doesn't intimidate me like the gold leaf of my leather-bound Bible: I can graffiti my reactions all over the text, safe in the knowledge that when I've read through this one I can afford to buy another and start all over again.

Perhaps all this talk about stuffing it down sofas or scribbling all over it sounds a shade too irreverent; it gets worse. Last night I read my Bible in the bath. It's not unusual for me to take a pile of books into the bathroom, but last night I was feeling in particular need of wisdom, so I was back in Proverbs. The water was cold by the end of Chapter Six, so I reluctantly reached out to exchange my Bible for a towel.

I missed.

I baptised my Bible . . . by immersion.

All is not lost. After a night on the radiator it has dried out. Admittedly, Revelation is now rather crinkly, and the first few chapters of Genesis no longer predate the flood, but apart from that it's perfectly readable. It's even acquired that impressive well-thumbed look that says, 'I belong to a saintly soul who spends hours in the Word.' The fact is it actually belongs to a slippery soul who soaks for too long in the bath, but no one need ever know.

Wednesday, 28 February

This morning we were all still in bed at five minutes to eight, hopelessly late for a school morning. We would still have been there at five past eight were it not for the fact that the phone rang. I shouted to the children to leave it because (a) we have no phone upstairs, (b) the alarm was still on downstairs and (c) the answerphone was on anyway.

Just as I was feeling unusually benevolent towards these last two items of technology, which had spared me the effort of early-morning communication, the doorbell rang.

Disgruntled, I went to open the door in my dressing-gown. It turned into a close encounter of the too cheerful kind with a wide-awake friend from church delivering something on his way to work. I felt as if I'd been caught with my rollers in (metaphorically speaking). My mood was not enhanced.

One phone message, one caller and it was not even 8 a.m.

Mornings like this only get worse. This one didn't hang about. All it took was a few cross words over a cereal bowl and *bang, flash, boom!*, it was 'up to your room this instant' time.

Too many demands, too little time, too many people, too early in the morning.

I made a note of the fact that it was only three days after half-term and already I was suffering from a shortage of fuse, but it didn't seem to help. I glanced at the clock and found myself thinking, *If I'm going to cry off from work today, I'd better ring now.* I just managed to catch the tail-end of this thought in time to challenge it.

'Cry off from work? You're not even ill,' I remonstrated with my reluctant inner self. 'The children aren't sick. All you've had is a few cross words over breakfast and you want to stay off work?'

Feebly I had to admit that while the idea appealed, it had a low credibility rating as far as excuses go: 'Sorry, I can't come in today. We fell out over the Benjamin Bunny bowl.'

I know it sounds ridiculous, but it doesn't *feel* ridiculous. It feels eminently reasonable to want to go back to bed just because of a few cross words. This is a symptom of 'final-straw syndrome', a condition brought on by having too many things to do and/or remember in too short a space of time. It's that state of mind where you are coping, but only just. All it will take is one more delay, one more interruption or one more unco-operative person and you feel that, frankly, you'd rather pass on today. Perhaps you could make a fresh start tomorrow?

But today is not an optional gift.

I leant heavily on the kitchen work surface, took a deep breath and prayed for the grace to start over. I prayed aloud. Loud enough for the aggrieved child upstairs to join in if she wished. 'Lord Jesus, please help us *all* this morning. Amen.' The emphasis was probably unfair but at least I'd made the first move. 'Breakfast's ready,' I called up. 'Let's start today again.'

Friday, 1 March

It's the end of the week and I haven't got the heart to start anything, not even a new month. I feel like I'm back where I was at the start of the year. This week has been particularly difficult: Year Eight took me apart on Monday, period three. Five pupils ended up in detention and I ended up in a sobbing heap on the sofa at home. On Wednesday we said a tearful farewell to Ruth and John, who have been our close friends and prayer partners and are now moving to the other end of the country. On Thursday I had to work in a different school, a possible place of employment for next September. It wasn't easy making a good impression when I'm not even sure if I want to be employed as a teacher next September.

On top of this my head is going round and round with the 'should we move house?' dilemma. Even my hormones weren't co-operating this week, so I shouldn't have attempted logical decision-making. I went round in circles: we can't afford to move unless I work, I hate work at the moment so we'll have to stay put, but I also want to move so I'll have to work, but I hate work . . . and so on and so on.

This is the first time we have ever considered basing our mortgage on our joint income. The responsibility of having to work in order to keep the roof over our heads seems awesome. I am all the more grateful to David for carrying it alone for such a long time and not at all sure if it's a responsibility I want to share.

I reached my lowest point at 5 p.m. on Tuesday when the phone rang. I was cooking tea and waiting for David to get in. Five in the evening is the second worst time of the day after early mornings. It was a friend who'd heard about the dreadful time I'd had at school on Monday. She heard the whole story first-hand and dropped round later with a small alcoholic beverage and a bar of chocolate to cheer me up. She did offer to pray as well!

It doesn't help my battered self-esteem that the papers are currently full of stories about disruptive pupils excluded from schools or assaulting teachers or other pupils. I pointed out to David that all of these infamous cases involve children in the year that I teach. He didn't comment but wisely offered to take me out for a meal tonight.

I've promised not to talk about school and he's promised not to talk about work. I hope we find something to say to each other.

Sunday, 3 March

It's been a good weekend. We enjoyed the pizza place on Friday night and I worked off my stress all day Saturday by tidying the house. I even made it out into the garden and planted some bulbs I'd found sprouting on the shed floor. Perhaps it's too late for them but I felt they deserved a chance.

By this evening I was in a more wholesome frame of mind, so I decided that Sunday evenings would be a good time to catch up on all my good intentions about regularly reading Bible stories to my children. Perhaps it's my own new Bible that has inspired me.

We started at the beginning (again) with the Garden of Eden. This was Matthew's choice of story, influenced no doubt by the fact that in his Children's Bible this story has a large, scary picture of the angel banishing Adam and Eve with a flaming sword. Anything with a sword is right up his street.

However, tonight he really did seem rather sorry for Adam and Eve once they'd been sent out of the garden. Aware of the enormous theological implications of the story, I tried (foolishly?) to draw out some of the lessons with leading questions.

'Why did God send them away?'

'They did a naughty thing.'

So far, so good.

'That's right, they disobeyed God. What should they do now?' (I was fishing for 'Repent,' 'Say sorry,' etc.).

There was a long pause, a puzzled frown and eventually a hopeful suggestion: 'Sneak back in when the angel isn't looking?'

The idea of Adam and Eve circumnavigating the purpose of God by sneaking around the angel made me smile. But my manoeuvrings this week as I've tried to settle unresolvable issues have been just as sneaky. Sorry, Lord.

Friday, 8 March – of sheep and camels

I thought we'd have another go at Bible stories tonight. We stuck to the simpler stuff this time. I chose the story of the lost sheep.

'Why did Jesus tell us this story?' I wondered aloud after we had read it. 'What did he want us to learn?'

'To look after our sheep' came the confident reply.

We live in a terraced house. There's no room for sheep.

Why do I bother? I wonder if it is really possible to bridge the gap between the world of the Bible and the world my children live in. Can I really make one seem relevant to the other?

This is a challenge currently facing us at church. I have been put in charge of a group reviewing our work with children, and one of the things that seem very important to all of us is that we must find ways to relate faith to life. If the Christianity we teach on Sundays has no connection with the children's Monday-to-Saturday world, then all we are offering is a relic, a souvenir religion.

A souvenir reminds you of something but is often useless. I have a souvenir from Egypt on my bookshelf, a gift from my well-travelled mother. It's a genuine leather camel whip.

'Just the thing for herding our camels up the avenue,' David remarked, somewhat tactlessly, when we received it.

If I am going to present the Bible as more relevant and useful than the souvenir on the shelf, then I'm going to have to do more than read stories and ask leading questions. 'Let the word of Christ dwell in you richly' (Colossians 3:16) reminds me that my Bible is not meant to live on my shelf (or down the back of the sofa) but in my life. 'And whatever you do,' it goes on to say, '. . . do it

'We live in a terraced house.
There's no room for sheep.'

(working, cooking, cleaning) all in the name of the Lord Jesus.'

Clearly my actions and attitudes need to speak louder than my story-telling.

Saturday, 9 March

The house dilemma rumbles on: our house is still on the market but no one has been around to see it lately. As if this wasn't sufficiently discouraging, someone has told me about another suitable house that might be just what we're looking for. My frustrations have spilled into my prayers, which have become shorter on worship and longer on petition.

This morning from the mouth of babes came a vivid description of my petulant attitude. Matthew had woken first, as usual, and far too early for a Saturday. He came into our bed, but after about ten minutes he began to wriggle restlessly, clearly irritated by his slumbering parents.

'Go and play, Matthew,' I said. 'I'll come in a while.'

Admitting defeat defiantly, he climbed out of bed but he couldn't resist one parting shot. 'Come in exactly a while!'

My sentiments precisely. When life doesn't comply with my timetable, the little child in me stamps her feet and dictates her terms to God. For his part, God has always come through for me in 'exactly a while', not perhaps at the time I'd dictated but not a moment too soon and not a moment too late. I know this from experience. Help me to remember it now, Lord.

Monday, 11 March

This evening the children were happily engaged in some covert craft activity for a full forty minutes after tea. They were making a gift for me; Mother's Day is imminent. I wasn't supposed to know about the gift they were creating but the peace and quiet downstairs, together with the disappearance upstairs of the scissors and Sellotape, rather gave the game away.

Before leaving for an evening meeting, David successfully coaxed them to tidy it all away so that I could come up and put them to bed. Tidying is Emma's forte, so she set to with enthusiasm. Unfortunately, the hand-made item got lost in the process. Matthew wailed with concern.

By this stage I was the only parent left in the house, so I was duly summoned and instructed to look for the something whose existence I wasn't supposed to know about.

'And when you find it, don't look at it,' Emma added for good measure.

I wasn't too sure how I was meant to know when I'd found it, but I did my best. It wasn't good enough. The search was fruitless.

'Daddy will find it,' I told a tearful Matthew as I tucked him into bed. 'At least he knows what he's looking for.'

Matthew wasn't much comforted and we had to pray for divine assistance in the matter. Later that evening, Daddy did indeed find the home-made cardboard creation, lurking behind the linen basket. It struck me that my efforts to find it, like my prayers about our house, had been fruitless and vague ('Do something . . . do anything'). Clearly what I need is a someone to come along and tell me what we're looking for, preferably the same someone who knows where to find it.

Wednesday, 13 March

I didn't make it in to work today. To be honest, I'm not at death's door; I've only got a cold, the sort that makes you feel as if you are wrapped in layers of cotton wool. I'm not even in pain. I am simply too disconnected from my senses to be safe in the classroom.

David is away again, so at least I can purloin all the pillows and sniff all night without disturbing anyone. Unfortunately, come the morning there will still only be me to get the kids off to school and drop the work off for my own classes.

I could hear the tone of self-justification in my voice when I rang in sick. I didn't actually hold my nose and stage a coughing fit but I was tempted.

Why do I think they won't believe me? I know I'm ill, but I still feel a bit pathetic having the day off for a mere cold. Still, at least no one can accuse me of having a Messiah complex. My talents with Year Eight are not unique and irreplaceable. Someone else can cope with them today.

Friday, 15 March

I shouldn't have bothered about feeling so guilty on Wednesday. My cold got a lot worse and I had to take yesterday off as well. This time a friend picked up my children for school and a pupil came and collected my work. I felt *bona fide* miserable all day, but I still spent a good part of it trying to plan a speaking engagement. It was a waste of effort. My capacity to think had clearly been diverted into the production of antibodies. I should have just gone to bed with a bar of chocolate.

I made it back to school today though and even felt fit enough to attend a lunchtime talk on healthy eating given by a dietician friend of mine. Among much excellent advice I made a few distressing discoveries: apparently I should be eating three or four portions of fruit or vegetables and drinking at least six pints of fluid every day; puddings ought to be a once-a-week treat; and there is no nutritional value whatever in a custard doughnut.

Given that I only have an occasional portion of

fruit or veg but eat puddings on a daily basis, I suppose I ought to be grateful I've only had a cold. It could have been scurvy. My response to the talk was to resolve to drink more, but six pints is an awful lot of visits to the bathroom. Still, all is not lost. On my way to the baker's this afternoon, I realised that the custard doughnut is, in fact, good for something. It's good for morale.

Tuesday, 19 March

Now that I am over my cold, it's the children's turn to be ill. Matthew has actually been complaining of a poorly tummy for some time. It started when the house went up for sale and his dad went away for a week. The symptoms come on suddenly every morning before school. I suspect that his unsettled tummy has more to do with the unsettled situation at home rather than anything more sinister. So far he's only been offered measured doses of sympathy.

But the complaints have been getting louder and more insistent, along the lines of 'Have you made an appointment at the doctor's yet, Mummy?' So this morning, in a fit of guilt and anxiety, I rushed him down to the surgery for the first available appointment, which happened to be in his school hours, much to his delight.

When his name was called he marched in ahead of

me, a picture of health, vitality and self-importance. He lapped up all the attention of the examination while I tried to look as if I wasn't the over-anxious mother I so obviously was. Even I thought he was a little too eager to explain how it hurt 'over there' when you pressed 'just here'.

The doctor quickly got the measure of the situation and, looking over Matthew's head, he handed me a prescription for some 'important pink medicine for poorly tums'. He all but winked at me as he explained that it could be taken 'as required'.

Thursday, 21 March

The phantom tummy pain lasted for a mere two doses. The pink stuff didn't taste half as nice as it looked and Matthew pronounced himself cured yesterday morning. Now that the tummy pain has gone he will have to rely on his lesser ailment as an attention-seeking tool. He has suffered from verrucas for the last six months and the unsightly sole of his left foot has proved very useful for warding off any unwelcome interference from his sister. He just whips off his sock and wields his foot in her face!

We have patiently applied foul-smelling potions and plasters to these nasty blemishes, the only effect of which has been to enhance their gruesome appearance. I did wonder if such a fetid left foot might be causing him emotional distress, but I shouldn't have worried. It has proved quite a conversation piece. This evening we introduced a new babysitter to the children and we knew she'd received immediate acceptance when Matthew sidled up to her grinning and said, 'Would you like to see my verrucas?'

Brenda, a grandmother small in stature but strong in spirit, didn't even flinch. Without a hint of surprise, she gave his worrisome warts due consideration and expressed appropriate appreciation. He then went happily off to bed.

Exit stage left (out of front door) two red-faced parents.

Monday, 25 March – on nutrition

Earlier this week one of my children mistook the wash basket on the landing for the waste basket in the bathroom. Easily done, I guess. This led to an innocent banana skin going through the entire wash process this morning. I discovered and removed a third of it at the sorting stage. I binned the next soggy portion as it came out of the washing-machine. I laid my hands on the final third as I emptied the tumble-drier.

In case you've never tumble-dried a banana skin, I should warn you that it comes out springy and crunchy like some huge crisp and dry spider, and it is not a pleasant thing to discover while sorting through one's smalls.

It's one thing to put a food item through a non-food utensil such as the washing-machine and quite another to put a non-food item through a food-preparation appliance. I am pleased to say I have also achieved this feat: I have microwaved toilet-roll tubes.

The helpful mothers from our toddler group had just collected a bin liner full of loo-roll tubes, all destined for some grand craft activity, when I received a letter informing me of the government's recommendation that loo-roll tubes should not be used for children's craft activities unless they have first been sterilised. This can be achieved by microwaving each individual tube on full power for ten seconds. When I was finally convinced that this letter wasn't a joke, I thought I ought to take my responsibilities as the toddler-group leader seriously, so I was faced with the prospect of microwaving almost a hundred loo-roll tubes one at a time. In my mind's eye I pictured David coming in from work with his usual enquiry, 'What's for tea?', dying on his lips. He has courageously faced many a weird creation in the ten years we've been married but has it come to this? Stuffed loo-roll? Loo-roll *à la* king?

The kitchen is not the scene of my greatest domestic triumphs. My cooking is edible but not outstanding and our nutritional standards leave me racked with guilt. I subscribe to the 'better a meal of vegetables where there is love' school of catering. I haven't actually got Proverbs 17:1 up on the wall above my cooker ('Better a dry crust with peace and quiet than a house full of feasting, with strife'), but I'm tempted.

However, there are always two choices for dinner in our house: take it or leave it. Greater love hath no husband for his wife than he devour her creations without complaint.

Occasionally David does raise a mild voice of protest. Last night I was writing out my bi-weekly menu prior to today's shopping trip. David was beside me reading the paper so, as he actually likes shopping for food, I asked him for some suggestions.

There was a long pause.

'You haven't made that slow-cooker casserole dish lately, have you?'

'Which one's that?' I said, perking up at the thought of recycling an old recipe.

'The one where you take half a field of potatoes, combine them with a watering can of cheese sauce, add three rashers of bacon and half a dozen thickly sliced and undercooked onions.'

'You mean "Cheese and Potato Casserole"?'

'Is that what it was?'

Realising his tone was hardly one of unrestrained enthusiasm, I asked him if he'd missed this delightful dish.

'No' was the unsurprising reply.

I think this particular recipe came from the era when I felt that if you were going to bother cooking one casserole you may as well cook five while you were at it. Our freezer overflowed with Pyrex dishes full of uninspiring cheese lumps, each one totally pallid except for a rare guest appearance made by a shy sliver of bacon.

Sometimes I feel driven by guilt to reform our family's diet. Yesterday, inspired by the vision of my children at school breaktime unwrapping some deliciously nutritious homemade goody diligently prepared for them by their loving mother (as opposed to their stressed-out working mother), I attempted flapjacks. I got out my *Healthy Eating for Children* recipe book, still as shiny and unused as the day I bought it, and found a recipe for 'fruit-filled flapjacks'. I set to with gusto; if the flapjacks didn't improve my children's health, they would at least soothe my conscience.

Somehow that melt-in-the-mouth consistency evaded me. My first attempt was rather more crumble-in-the-hand, but I wasn't put off. My second effort produced concrete slabs, ideal for extracting those wobbly little milk teeth. Refusing to be beaten, my third and final attempt was perfect – moist and chewy, the ideal consistency.

I was delighted . . . until I came to take the slices out of the baking tray. Then I discovered that each piece of flapjack came with its own unique coating of non-stick liner.

Exit to outside bin one serving of flapjacks and one ruined baking tray.

Annoyingly (for people like me), there are no short-cuts to good nutrition. This afternoon Matthew reminded me of this when he rushed in from outside saying, 'Mummy, come quick, there's leeks in the garden.'

Having never planted anything so wholesome and nutritious as a leek, I was intrigued by the possibility of home-grown vegetables springing up with zero effort on my part.

I was disappointed. On reaching the garden Matthew pointed to a large puddle forming under the base of a flowerpot he'd over-watered.

'Oh, *those* sorts of leaks!'

How often I long for quick fixes, but there's no such thing as instant nutrition, nor can I achieve microwaved maturity. I want an overnight response from God, but his plans are much more long-term.

Tuesday, 26 March

Still no one has been around to see the house. Meanwhile two new purchasing possibilities have arisen: one is a house in our street and the other is a large, rather run-down house in the right area. I'd need a diploma in home decorating if we took on the second of these two options, but neither will become a reality if we can't sell our house. I keep trying to look round corners into the future, but God's giving nothing away. Whenever some new possibility arises I think, *Perhaps this is it, perhaps this is what we were meant to wait for*, but without a buyer we are going nowhere. It's all rather got on top of me this month.

Wednesday, 27 March

The school holidays are almost here and I'm so looking forward to the break from the weekly routine. On the home front my two most wearisome tasks are public relations and consumer affairs – i.e., squabbling siblings and the shopping. The school holidays don't offer any let-up from these particular two pressures, but at least they can be conducted without the restraining influence of the twice daily school run and the complication of my teaching timetable. We can all lounge around in our pyjamas till 10 a.m. if we please, and after having to step out into the raw cold at some much earlier hour for weeks on end, this will feel wonderfully wicked.

Life in the classroom has been an exhausting experience this term. My diplomatic and arbitration skills have been regularly stretched to their limit by the more disruptive children in my classes. The fact of living and working in a secular society is also a constant challenge. When we had a 'Readathon' week over half the children brought in 'Point Horror' stories from choice. When I was off sick two weeks ago, I set my class the story title 'Reaction'. They had to write a story in which the main character had some news to tell. Ninety-five per cent of the girls wrote about telling their parents they were pregnant.

I teach twelve-year-olds.

I am left with the discouraging feeling that I am facing a cultural mountain and all I can do is roll marbles at it. Still, 'if you have faith as small as a mustard seed, you can say to this mountain . . .' It feels very hard to believe that on some days in school, and were I not faithfully prayed for by a dear lady in church, I think I would have given up weeks ago.

Thursday, 28 March

The weekend approaches and not a moment too soon. I should have self-certified for sheer weariness today. Instead I dragged myself into school, in body if not in spirit, and found myself in a typical staffroom conversation.

'What year do you teach?' my colleague enquired.

I heard the question; I understood the question; but my mind and mouth refused to co-ordinate, so I stuttered out the only fact I was sure about. 'I'm Sheila Bridge,' I said with a winning smile. I might as well have added, 'And I'm from another planet,' for all the sense I was making!

Never mind, the weekend beckons and, behind it, another Monday and another Monday and another Monday.

Easter is coming up over the horizon. I need to be

lifted out of my dull routine and to hear again the refreshing surprise of the Risen Jesus reminding me that this long journey isn't a meaningless meander but a definite journey to a joyful destination: heaven itself. Sometimes I feel impatient and am tempted to ask, like a small child on a long journey, 'Are we nearly there yet, Lord?' And, please, when we get there, could there be no Mondays in heaven?

Saturday, 30 March

I made it to the holidays! Yesterday was a good day. First, the tax-man sent me back all the money he should not have been taking off me in the first place for the last six months. Second, I wrote an article and, third, I successfully e-mailed it to the correct destination. We haven't had the technology to do this for very long, so it counts as a triumph. Our 'service provider' (the people who take our money to connect us to the Internet) runs a free phone help-line for any would-be surfers who've lost their way. I must have spent at least three hours this month talking to a series of helpful Irishmen: Shaun, Patrick and Declan were not the least patronising and never expressed any surprise at my ignorance, which was very decent of them. I was just wondering why Irishmen seem to have cornered the job market in computer help-line services when it finally dawned on me that I was probably ringing Ireland. Thank goodness it was free.

Today we are down at my mum's in Kent, and we are going over to see our friends in their new home (the ones we said farewell to at the end of February). The daffodils are already out here. Spring is on the way. It's not been an easy month, but with the prospect of a break ahead, I can feel my spirit lifting. Here's to April.

Monday, 1 April

The children were up before us this morning and seemed unusually keen for us to come down for breakfast. We soon discovered why: the milk was blue and the inner packets of all the cereal boxes had been switched round. What a wheeze! They were delighted and chortled about their cleverness for the rest of the morning.

The week ahead is rather overloaded with domestic chores. We are going away to Spring Harvest on Thursday with a whole gang of friends from church, so there's plenty of shopping, washing and packing to keep me occupied. Matthew also needs new school shoes.

My preoccupations remain the same: should we keep the house on the market or should we give up and accept the situation? David and I have talked about it and agreed to give the matter special prayer while we are away and then pool our conclusions. My feeling at the moment is that we should drop the price and move anywhere bigger; David thinks we should stay put. If we reach the same conclusion, I'll be amazed.

I'm still rather keen to buy the run-down property, on the basis that we could afford it without me having to work. I talked this option over with a friend yesterday. She has moved house twice in six years, extensively rearranging both properties. I was expecting to amuse her with our plans to do the same.

She didn't laugh. She didn't even smile . . . A warning bell sounded in my head. Perhaps I shouldn't insist on my own way. After all, I might not know what's good for me.

Thursday, 4 April

We've arrived at Butlin's, Skegness, for the annual extravaganza of Christian teaching, praise, worship, fellowship and yet more teaching that is known as Spring Harvest. We also plan to do a fair bit of swimming. The pool is the best bit, according to Emma.

I have forgotten everything I was told to bring: mugs (so we'll have to make do with Butlin's teacups), breakfast cereal (so we'll have to go to the shop), my special pillow (so my head will fall off after three nights) and Emma's pyjamas.

Emma was most indignant about the final oversight and broadcast my shortcomings to the rest of our party. She cheered up when I bought her a brand-new pair at the Butlin's Boutique, but my reputation for efficiency had already been dented. Having cooked our first meal here, I can see that it won't be the only part of my reputation to suffer. Ours is the middle chalet in a row of five chalets occupied by us and four other families from our church. There are only about ten paces between one front door and the next. All the kids play football outside until their mothers call them in for their meals. This evening my kids were the last ones out there, and eventually they gave up on the football and enquired about the progress of their supper. 'An unfamiliar oven' was my excuse for the singular lack of delicious cooking smells from our quarters. We ate our undercooked meal in a rush and left the dishes unwashed in order to get out in time for the first session.

Sunday, 7 April – Easter Day

The last four days have been a whirl of activity. We've averaged four sessions a day, and I've been swimming so often I ought to be porous. The kids have enjoyed their groups as much as the pool, and David and I have enjoyed all the opportunities for adult input. By yesterday I ran out of excuses for the inefficient catering. I eventually got the hang of the oven – so much so that I burnt the lasagne and everyone knew when tea was ready at our place.

As we'd agreed, David and I had been keeping

our ears pinned back for a response from God regarding our housing dilemma. Today, day four, was the first chance we had to pool our conclusions. Several of the sessions I'd attended had addressed much deeper issues than the small matter of our house. I had been challenged, rebuked, comforted, encouraged, reinvigorated . . . and that was just on Friday!

I came away from the Bible readings in Galatians excited that I had a righteousness that was not of my own making; it was a gift from God. This was really good news to someone emerging from a dark period of doubt. Since my bathtime meditation at Christmas my faith has felt weak. As a well-brought-up evangelical, I'd been using the vigour of my faith as a kind of measure of my standing as a Christian. But this is to make faith into a work, not a gift, a grace from God. What I got from God out of Galatians is that God graciously calls me his delightful child regardless of how I feel about myself or the strength of my faith.

Yippee! I am out of the bath at last. I'm dressed in the team colours and selected for the team even though my game's not up to much. I feel deeply reassured.

I have also been challenged about my work. Part of my negative attitude towards this job has stemmed from the way it was given to me. Back in September a ex-colleague who happened to know I lived near his school realised that I could possibly plug the gaps in his timetable. I turned down the opportunity twice.

'If you really want me to teach, Lord, then he'll have to come back and ask me again,' I reasoned.

Less than a week later, he did. 'And could you start next week?' he added for good measure.

It was more than a shock to be plunged back into secondary teaching after five years' absence from the classroom. It was terrifying, exhausting and exhilarating all at the same time. The whole thing knocked me for six spiritually. Had I heard God wrong? Was it a big mistake?

Admittedly, the experience has taught me a lot about unconditional love: God's unconditional love for difficult kids, mind you, not my love for them. It humbles me to think that God loves people who are so rude, unco-operative and downright aggressive. I've really tried to love them, but I struggle with the constraints of the role. I have to teach them about speech marks and paragraphs when what they really need is someone to tell them about the things that really matter in life: love, God and respect.

What bothers me most about work at the moment is the feeling that I will have to continue with it if we are ever to move. It feels so dispiriting to be doing it only for the money. But one evening one of the speakers talked about how work was God's idea and how we shouldn't rate some parts of our lives as 'spiritual' and therefore good, and others, such as work, as 'unspiritual' and therefore bad. Like Joseph in Egypt, we have to make the most of every situation, to excel in the prison as much as in the palace.

I still feel that this vocation is my personal prison, but as someone once said, probably a stern-faced evangelical, 'Being happy is not a yardstick for whether or not you are in God's will and fulfilling his purposes.' Disappointing but true. I guess I'll just have to make the best of it.

Finally, about the house dilemma: David and I agreed, although we never saw it written in letters of gold across the sky, that God would have us do nothing and wait. All our efforts to sell have come to nothing and it feels as if we have been scheming a detour that doesn't fit in with God's bigger plan. We've no idea what that plan is, but we've agreed to take the house off the market and just wait. We don't know what for or for how long, but until the light changes to green we shall just have to wait.

Not exactly the conclusion I'd hoped for, but after all the other encouragements of the last few days it's getting easier to concede that God knows better than I do.

Monday, 8 April

The children deserved to be sick today but thankfully they weren't. Yesterday they consumed more chocolate in one day than they usually have in a week. Chocolate eggs and empty tombs – it's a tenuous link. I've never felt really sure about why it is that we eat oval confectionery at this time of year.

When the kids ask me, 'When will it be Easter?' I know their enquiry has more to do with the anticipation of calories rather than the joyful celebration of a glorious truth. What is a Christian parent to do? If we don't give them chocolate eggs/bunnies/chickens, we sour the celebrations by being mean-minded misers. If we do give them copious quantities of chocolate, it can work against us. After all, it's hard enough for a small child to focus on the real meaning of Easter at any time, let alone when he has two distracting fistfuls of warm, melting chocolate to occupy him.

Last year we concentrated on joy. We went out and did something quite silly with several other families who were similarly inclined. Early on Easter Sunday morning, even before breakfast if I remember rightly, we took the children egg-rolling.

Egg-rolling is a sport that requires a local steep and preferably grassy slope. The aim is to roll one's hard-boiled and painted eggs down the incline and see whose reaches the bottom first and/or stays intact for the longest.

We were serious competitors. We even varnished the eggs to cut down surface friction and increase the durability of our entrants!

The adults had a wonderful time: charging up and down hillsides and shouting encouragement at

'We were serious competitors'

inanimate objects proved to be the perfect diversion from mundane routine. The kids had a good time too. We finished up by sending them on an egg hunt, and the harvest of eggs gathered was consumed before we'd got back to base. We adults then greeted the Easter dawn with a breakfast of coffee and chocolate.

I hope egg-rolling doesn't have any dire pagan connection. Eggs, new life, spring: they all get muddled in with the Easter festival. Children's BBC have just run a competition to design an Easter card featuring dinosaur eggs. How's that for an almighty muddle of theology and geology? At least if we roll our eggs, we can make slight connections with the rolling away of a certain stone.

This year at Spring Harvest the children have had so much input they would hardly have noticed Easter if it hadn't been for the chocolate. I didn't bother giving any explanations. When all the calories have been consumed, when sticky hands and faces have been wiped, I hope it will be their sense of joy and delight, hope and surprise, that remains their abiding memory of the celebration.

Wednesday, 10 April

We came home yesterday to the depressing discovery that not only had we forgotten to take vital items with us to Spring Harvest but we'd also forgotten to bring several significant items home, the most significant being Matthew's school shoes, the brand-new pair I'd gone out and paid £35 for the day before we went away. The bright, shiny black pair with the Velcro fastening and the magic picture that appeared as your feet got hot.

He'd been wearing his tatty old trainers on our last day away and the school shoes had been shoved under the bed in the chalet, which is where they stayed.

My first idea was that as I'd paid by credit card, they'd be covered by insurance. No chance: it only covers items over £50. My second idea was to ring Butlin's Lost Property. I got a very helpful lady who said, 'Hold on a minute, dear,' in such a hopeful tone of voice I thought she'd have them. She was away so long I thought she'd actually gone to the chalet to check. She came back to say she had a black pair of size 11s (hooray!). Adult size 11s, that is (boo!). She suggested I try later in the week. I hope the trainers will last that long.

Saturday, 13 April – on buying clothes

I tried the lady at Butlin's again yesterday, but Matthew's shoes still haven't appeared. I'm harbouring unChristian thoughts towards whoever moved into our chalet after we moved out. Resigned to their loss, we went out and replaced them today with some sandals that cost half the price. Let's hope summer arrives soon.

I couldn't find Velcro sandals, so he'll have to cope with a buckle, which is a bit of a shame because he's still not very motivated when it comes to dressing himself, and anything that makes it harder doesn't help. He wasn't too keen on the sandals. He really wanted another pair with an impressive magic picture, but we can't afford the same again. Thankfully, he's not really particular about what he wears. I know shopping for clothes with some children can be a nightmare.

There are definitely 'frilly' girls and 'unfrilly' girls, and woe betide you if you try to persuade your frilly filly into some sensible trousers even if you are going for a family hike over Dartmoor. Likewise there are some 'cool dude' guys and some 'couldn't care less' guys. Matthew usually comes into the second category and Emma isn't too fussy either.

Perhaps they are laid-back about it because I've never made clothes into an issue. I've learnt that clothes aren't usually worth an argument. When their earliest attempts to dress themselves resulted in them coming down for breakfast wearing wellies, shorts and a tea-cosy on their head, I thought it was best not to comment. The tricky bit was when they wanted to go outside and play wearing the same gear on a cold winter day. This is where opinion divides into two streams of thought: either 'make them wear a coat' or 'leave them to work it out for themselves'. Being the totally consistent parent that I am, I agree with both views. It's a fact that while some children will whine with cold but steadfastly refuse to do anything about it, others will develop peculiar internal thermostats. Our little friend Emily was a good example of this. Emily could be guaranteed to arrive at school in mid-summer, beetroot-red in the face, wearing woolly tights and a thick jumper. In winter she would insist on summer frocks. Her mother wisely decided that it was simply best not to let this bother you. After all, it never bothered Emily.

The sorts of things that trouble children about clothes are rarely the same things that trouble you. I don't know what worried Matthew about his new sandals today, but he wasn't at all keen on them.

A few years ago I couldn't persuade Emma *not* to wear an over-sized pair of bright orange sunglasses. She had decided that, as Mummy and Daddy both wore glasses, why shouldn't she? As she had removed the black plastic lenses and I couldn't see that they were doing her any harm, I opted for the policy of ignoring them, knowing that the more I didn't want her to wear them, the more she would insist. This policy worked . . . eventually. She wore them for three weeks, everywhere we went from dawn to dusk. People even began to compliment me on my adventurous choice of spectacles.

I'm glad I didn't fight it. Children rarely co-operate with ploys that suit parents, or if they do, they carry the policy to a bizarre but logical extreme. A friend of mine gave me a great illustration of this.

She has twins, and in order to help people tell them apart she hit upon the idea of colour-coding their clothing: lemon-yellows for Lucy and rosy-reds for Rachel. All went well, if somewhat expensively, until the day she presented them with a box of multicoloured tissues and asked them both to blow their noses. She disappeared under a shower of tissues as both girls rifled through the box looking for a rosy-red for Rachel and a lemon-yellow for Lucy!

Never in the field of human conflict have so many parents fallen out so often with their children as over a pair of trainers. 'He said he'd wear them in the shop and now we've got home he says they are gross.' I hope Matthew doesn't feel that bad about his sandals.

Monday, 15 April

Guess what came in the post this morning? Yep, Matthew's size 11 black shoes with the magic picture. He'd already left for school wearing the replacement pair. Grrr!

Wednesday, 17 April

The first couple of days back in the classroom haven't been too bad. It's also good to have a little more personal space at home now that my own kids are at school again. I feel I need at least a week to get back into my stride after a week with them both at home.

Emma finally lost one of her wobbly teeth last night. It had been wobbly for weeks, and she was eventually parted from it (for safety's sake) amid much screaming, wailing and shedding of blood. For something so wobbly, it hung on with remarkable tenacity.

Not five minutes later, she lost the same tooth all over again. She had placed it on the kitchen work surface (yuck!) to save it for the tooth fairy later. It disappeared goodness knows where during the after-tea tidy-up.

Teeth, it seems, are traumatic in both their arrival and departure. I'll bet this particular tooth was the same one that had given us so much misery when she first cut it at seven months old. Now seven years later its departure left a trail of misery all the way up the stairs to bed. A tear-stained note was penned for the tooth fairy, which Mummy had to validate with her signature ('It did come out, honestly it did'). I was left to decide whether the tooth fairy is a heartless mercenary who simply pays out for collected ivory – i.e., 'No pearlies, no pennies' – or a compassionate being who compensates small children for the pain of extraction.

I opted for the latter and paid up as usual.

Friday, 19 April

Matthew's phantom tummy pain is back. I had

hoped the pink medicine he had back in March had seen it off, but this week he didn't want to go to school again. Someone said to me that small children get 'headaches' in their tummies, which set me wondering what might be giving Matthew a headache.

I knew his anxiety was related to school, so when he brought back a reading book all about a little lad, Frankie, who wept an ocean of tears on his first day at school, I waited for a good moment to read it to him.

We were talking about Frankie's fears when Matthew confided: 'I work very hard at school. I *musn't* be last and I *musn't* make mistakes.'

I reassured him that I knew he worked hard, and I also suggested to him that mistakes didn't matter so very much.

He looked at me appalled. 'But my friend Michael never finished his work and he made lots of mistakes and now he's been sent to another school,' his response tumbled out.

This was the first I had heard about Michael leaving. Obviously no explanation had been given as to why he had left and Matthew had jumped to an 'obvious' conclusion: he wasn't clever enough.

'People don't have to leave school just because they make mistakes,' I told him. He looked unconvinced and my heart went out to him. He's only four and already failure is like a black shadow spurring him on. How will I convince him that his value is not measured by his SATS test? Given the educational system he's yet to pass through, I suspect this will not be the last time I have to remind him that success is not measured uniquely by gold stars, credits or exam grades.

Monday, 22 April

It's the start of another week and I'm feeling more on edge than usual. My period is late and I'm wondering if God had something entirely different in mind when he said, 'Wait.' We have more or less decided that we are happy with the two children we've got, thank you very much. I can't see that I'd be a better mother with three to cope with – quite the reverse. I know I'd struggle. Sometimes I feel sad about them not having a same-sex sibling because I enjoy having a sister, but I have to remind myself that I didn't enjoy having a big sister when I was a child and I'm sure she felt the same about me. Our poor parents – when I remember the rows I feel for them.

I wouldn't be devastated if I was pregnant. I could probably even be pleased. Physically it would be hard-going but we'd manage somehow. It seems such a daunting decision, to have third child; a mistake would be a relief in a way, as it would lift the burden of decision-making. As it is, we are just on the verge of deciding how to resolve our fertility dilemma permanently. Our grandmothers never had this choice. But choice isn't easy; it feels like an awesome responsibility.

'Never have three,' my mother used to say to me. 'Someone's always left out.' This rather negative view of the situation wasn't exactly encouraging for me, the third child in her threesome. Perhaps she only said it when we rowed and who can blame her? I console myself with the fact that I was very much a planned baby, the result of a late surge of maternal feelings.

Friends with three kids have told me it's great, not so intense as the rivalry between a twosome, and I believe them. I just don't like odd numbers. If I can't stop at two, perhaps I should have four. But then again four feels like six more than three, so I've been told. Maybe not.

Quit while you're ahead, that's my policy. I have a girl and a boy. They don't come in any other variety. But we shall see what this week brings.

Thursday, 25 April

Yesterday was dreadful in the classroom. I put six kids in detention for tomorrow night and I had to send two out to the withdrawal room (solitary confinement in the dining room).

I had kept my temper under control through it all until almost the end, then one child who had ignored me the whole lesson stopped ignoring me and started swearing at me. I blew my stack.

I still had a face like thunder when I got home, only to be greeted by my neighbour, who told me that part of his back wall had been damaged. I went to inspect and it was perfectly obvious that it was malicious damage done by kids too thick to work out from the back of our row of terraced houses which one belonged to 'Miss'. I only live 300 yards from the school, so I expect to be recognised by the kids as they go past the house on their way to the chip shop, but damaging my neighbour's property was not on. I knew the culprits – I'd seen them loitering with intent – so I rang the school. The deputy head was very supportive but the whole episode depresses me. It's one thing to be hassled in working hours but quite another to be harassed in your own home.

How did you do it, Lord? How did you manage not to storm off in a huff when you were spat at, reviled and abused? I find it hard to react lovingly when I'm merely sworn at. Help me to find in my heart some of your love for these kids.

Saturday, 27 April

I went to help out at a children's party today. It wasn't your average sausages-on-sticks affair. This was a waistcoat party, hosted by my arty-crafty friend Sarah. Sarah runs her own business making wooden toys. She has taught herself all sorts of obscure crafts; her current project is learning to make stained-glass windows. She's on the school PTA but is seriously considering home-educating her two girls. She teaches gym in her spare time. She eats chocolate by the pound and doesn't get fat . . . If I didn't like her so much, I'd hate her! She even managed to arrange her children's birthdays efficiently – she had both her girls on the same day, two years apart.

So today was Jessica's and Sophie's birthday and the waistcoat party bit was for Jessica and seven of her friends. Sarah had prepared the fabric pieces for eight waistcoats; all the girls had to do was select their trimmings and sew them up. My part in this enterprise was to turn up with my sewing machine and sew. The girls lost interest rather early, so Sarah and I had to leave them stuffing their faces at the tea table while we speed-sewed four waistcoats each. They were all very proud of their work when their mummies arrived.

'Not so successful as last year's paint-your-own-T-shirt party,' Sarah concluded when it was all over. I thought it was brilliant. Full marks for ambition. The only problem is what do you do next year?

Monday, 29 April

It's been exam week for Year Eight this week. What a relief. My little horrors have had to spend six hours a day sitting in silence in the gym, chewing their pencils and scribbling their answers. All I have had to do is walk quietly up and down the rows, giving out paper and sorting out problems. Some of them don't seem to understand what an exam is. They ask you what a question means and look really offended when you explain that you can't help them ('You mean I've got to do this on my own?').

I have not gloated, not even for a moment. They have all looked quite sorry for themselves and I have found it helpful to look up and down the rows and pray for each child by name. Maybe no one has ever prayed for those children before except Maureen. Maureen is the reason I'm still here. She also lives near the school and when she heard I was to teach there she took a copy of my timetable and offered to pray for me. She's prayed for the badly behaved boys and the girl with the panic attacks and she's never even seen any of them. She does it all so lovingly, it's not hard to believe her prayers will be answered – at least it's not hard today when they are all sitting silently in rows.

Tuesday, 30 April – of family planning

Relief of another kind came this morning. I'm not pregnant. I don't feel at all disappointed, so that tells me something, doesn't it? I think it's time we made a joint appointment at a Family Planning Clinic. They are such embarrassing places – going into one is like wearing a big badge that says, 'I have sex,' and I'm not so liberated as to be able to do this comfortably. I'll shout hooray for the Health Service, regular smear tests and free contraceptives, but I'd prefer to do so with a paper bag on my head.

When/if I do actually go to the clinic, I have to consciously tell myself that this is a right and reasonable place to be. Even so, I can't help watching the door in case anyone I know walks in and sometimes someone does.

The other problem I've had with clinics has been getting past the receptionist. My first experience was so dreadful, it was a wonder I ever went back.

I had walked into a large, silent room where a receptionist was sitting in the middle of a square arrangement of chairs on which were an assortment of patients and magazines. The receptionist was just deaf enough not to catch my name the first time. So, having announced my name to the whole waiting room, I sat down and buried my head in a magazine. When I finally looked up, it was straight into the face of a pupil from the school where I taught.

She knew who I was. I knew who she was. I knew she was under sixteen and she knew that I knew.

We faced each other in silence. I could hardly have said anything reassuring or otherwise, and particularly not while the poor girl was reeling under the revelation that 'Miss' had sex too.

She must have sat there worrying whether I would tell. I didn't. She can't have told on me either because later that same year, when I told my class of sixteen-year-olds that I was leaving to have the baby that had been so obviously widening my waistline (so much for family planning), they reacted with silent shock and amazement.

Teenagers are funny creatures. They give the impression they know all about sex, and perhaps they do, but any discreet reference to your own normal, healthy sexuality and they squirm with embarrassment.

Not long after this we moved to a new area and I gave up teaching, so I thought it was safe to return to a FPC. At the first visit I filled in all the usual information on the file they retrieve at every subsequent visit.

So far, so good.

On my next visit I went in and gave my name.

'We need your number to find your file,' I was told.

'I didn't know I had a number.'

After much muttering and tutting the file was somehow found. By the next visit I had diligently rehearsed my number. The clinic had moved to a smart new building and I leant across the wide reception desk and hissed, '626,' out of the side of my mouth.

The receptionist was unimpressed. 'We've changed the system,' she said. 'We only need your name now.'

At that moment the automatically opening doors closed . . . terminally. Unable to leave the scene of my embarrassment, I hung around long enough to get a card with all my pertinent details printed inside and then I left by the fire escape.

By the next visit I was all prepared. I'd remembered my card; all I had to do was hand it over. I wouldn't have to say a thing. I passed it to the receptionist. She opened it, looked at it, looked at me and there was a long pause.

There, obliterating all the words in thick blue felt pen (you can never find a Biro when you need one), was a shopping list: 'milk, eggs, flour, cheese'.

I suspect that written requests for such items at Family Planning Clinics are somewhat rare, the contraceptive value of grocery products being as yet unproven.

There was no easy way out. I felt like reciting my name, my number, my gynaecological history, the number of my house, my husband's name, the name of my psychiatrist . . . Instead I gave up.

Perhaps we'll go to the doctor instead. At least he knows who we are and it'll save me having to remember.

Wednesday, 1 May

I saw one of those strange 3D pictures today in town, the ones which are a meaningless mess of blobs and colours that you have to stand and stare at until it feels as if your eyes are about to pop out of your head. I've tried several times to make out the 3D image, but you can feel very conspicuous standing in a shop going cross-eyed and squinting with effort. The other method is to start with your nose on the picture and then slowly step back several paces while staring straight ahead, but this kind of behaviour in a public place qualifies you as seriously loopy.

Today, however, I saw the picture within a picture. I looked across and there it was. I don't know if it was a trick of the light or the angle of the picture, but suddenly I could just make out the shadowy 3D image embedded in the coloured shapes. I couldn't see what it was, mind you, but I could see it was a picture of something. A layer of meaning in a different dimension all of its own.

Faith seems a bit like that: a layer of meaning in a dimension all of its own. Lately my life has felt like a meaningless mess of blobs and colours and I have been staring hard at it, trying to work out what it's all about. Faith is a bit like putting on a pair of glasses that allow you to see the shadowy image embedded in the picture. Sometimes it's hard to make out what the image is meant to be but I get the occasional glimpse and this gives me hope.

Help me to find my faith specs today, Lord.

Sunday, 5 May

Yesterday we came down to Mum's to celebrate the eightieth birthday of Grandpa Bill (Dr William Young to give him his full title).

'Ten years past my sell-by date,' he joked, referring to the biblical average.

'Count the "happies", not the birthdays,' my sister had written in her card.

The cards were an important part of the evening's entertainment, as Mum had asked each of us to enclose in our cards a poem written in honour of the occasion. I can't write poetry to save my life, so David had written a limerick. It was better than anything I could have done, but it was still a poor effort compared to the witty doggerel produced by several other family members.

After the poems we put on a *This is Your Life* show for him, with his children and grandchildren doing walk-on impressions of him from his earlier life. We celebrated his exploits in the medical field, the rugby field and the mission field, not to mention the Norfolk Broads and his success as an author. The evening ended with a prayer of thanksgiving for 'Gramps' before he went off to bed muttering modestly, 'Don't believe a word of it,' to anyone who'd listen.

This morning Matthew solemnly informed Grandpa that he'd be an inch taller now he'd had a birthday. Matthew believes that you only grow on your birthday. This opinion first came to light when I was coaxing him to eat vegetables with the well-worn line 'You won't get big and strong if you don't eat your peas.'

'Peas don't make you grow,' he retorted. 'Birthdays do!'

'Perhaps Grandpa was so tall on account of his many birthdays.'

Perhaps Grandpa was so tall on account of his many birthdays? When you are only three foot something this theory seems plausible. If it were true, Grandpa would now be a terrifying eight foot three inches, assuming he started out with the average twenty inches at birth.

But there is a sense in which Grandpa hasn't stopped growing. I peeked into the wide-margin Bible my mother bought him only last year and was impressed with how many observations had already been recorded on so many pages.

'Keeping looking up,' he often encourages us. Perhaps Grandpa's stature at eighty, both physical and spiritual, has more to do with his inner posture and the certainty of his final destination than any of his outward achievements.

It will be Mum's and Bill's third wedding anniversary later this month. They got together after a whirlwind romance of about two weeks. Mum had been on her own for five years after Dad died before Bill came on the scene. I wasn't at all worried about the speed of their courtship. After all, if you've already clocked up eighty years of married life between you, you ought to know what you're looking for. Nor did the idea of a stepfather bother me. I've always felt that to remarry after a bereavement is somewhat of a compliment to your first partner; marriage can't have been at all bad if you are happy to repeat the experience.

But it was a strange role reversal, watching the

older generation fall in love. On their first date Mum was in a complete dither, terrified that he'd actually turn up to take her out and equally terrified that he wouldn't!

At the time, David and I felt like a jaded old married couple, weighed down with work, a mortgage, church responsibilities and small children, while these OAPs behaved like a pair of spring chickens, frolicking about the countryside with nothing more urgent than the next cream tea on their minds.

Once plans began to be laid for a wedding Mum, of course, found plenty to occupy her mind. What would she wear? Where would they marry? And who would be the bridesmaids? The choice of her three granddaughters for that last duty delighted them all. This made me the daughter of the bride and the mother of a bridesmaid, a fairly stressful position, especially when with three weeks to go Matthew came down with chicken pox. The illness has a two-week incubation period, so I was facing the possibility of Emma coming down with it in time for the wedding. In that same week Emma's front tooth started to wobble and she came into contact with 'slapped face' virus. This was a new one on me, but apparently it was likely to result in a red face and swollen hands and feet. Overcome with mild hysteria, I had a vision of two angelic little bridesmaids, my nieces, and one spotty little troll with huge hands and no front teeth, my daughter! Thankfully none of these dire possibilities came about.

If presenting Emma in good shape was one priority, my attire was the next. Foolishly I attempted to make my own outfit. Given that I have a love–hate relationship with my sewing machine and attempted a garment well beyond the reach of my competence, the disaster that resulted was no surprise.

The great day dawned at last and somehow we arrived at the church well dressed and in our right minds – almost. Despite endless coaching to the contrary, Matthew kept insisting that Grandma was marrying a monkey. Hoping he wouldn't declare this fact as a due impediment at the wrong moment during the service, I went armed with several packets of chocolate buttons. These were gleefully consumed in comparative silence. With all that chocolate he must have concluded that weddings were a good idea.

As they left for their honeymoon later in the day, I tucked some strawberry lip balm into Mum's bag, labelled 'For the sweetest kisses'. Love is, of course, more than just kisses but the flavour of 'in-loveness' had done us all good.

Since then they have travelled together for three years and over several thousand miles as Mum is a bit of a globe-trotter. They have also survived illnesses, operations and set-backs. They may have felt they already knew all there was to know about marriage, but I have a feeling they've been learning some more: more love, more patience, more tolerance and more tenderness.

I hope I'm still learning when I get to their age.

Monday, 6 May

This morning Matthew asked me, 'How many days till May is over?'

While I was still calculating the correct response, he followed up with another question that revealed the reason for his sudden interest in the calendar.

'Is it July next?'

He will be five in July. I had to break it to him gently that we still had most of May and all of June to get through. He wasn't very impressed. I think the weekend birthday celebrations for Grandpa have put him in the mood for his birthday. He likes to plan his party three months in advance: the guest list, the games and the cake. Last year he wanted a pirate-ship cake from Easter to mid-July, then changed his mind at the last moment. I don't mind so much anticipation – it's a big deal when you're only five. I only hope he doesn't start inviting people now.

Tuesday, 7 May

The great space debate continues. Space as in living space and storage space. We are still suffering from a shortage of both. In response to God's directive to wait we took our house off the market after Easter but the place doesn't get any bigger by itself.

Something has to be done. I'd offer to live in the garage if I thought it would help.

On a more realistic note, I thought of building a dining room across the back of the house and putting a porch on the front with room for a loo. I mentioned the idea to David this evening.

His eyes lit up with pound signs.

'But think of all the moving expenses we've saved,' I appealed.

He reached for his calculator and the initial computations looked promising but then he had second thoughts: 'Is it really what we want?' 'It's still a lot of money.' 'We don't know any builders.' Soon the idea was well buried under a pile of practical objections. Never mind, perhaps I'll mention it again next week when he's had time to mull it over.

Saturday, 11 May

Now that I've got used to the fact that we are not selling the house I am beginning to appreciate some of the benefits of staying put: namely our neighbours, who came to my rescue several times today.

As it was raining, the kids and I had decided to do some baking. This may sound like a very homely and old-fashioned activity, but it isn't. I can't be doing with all that whisking, folding and rubbing. I just throw everything in the food processor and press the buttons. If it isn't an all-in-one recipe to start off with, it is by the time I've finished with it.

All the kids get to do is break the eggs, press the buttons and lick the bowl. On my more tolerant days they also get to weigh the flour. They like the licking the bowl bit best. This is because they have learnt that my cakes invariably taste better before they are put into the oven.

This rosy-hued scene of domestic bliss began with a fraught search for the square cake tin, which had disappeared only because I had determined to try an unfamiliar recipe which required a square tin. Refusing to give up, I dispatched the children to borrow one from the neighbours and, thus equipped, we pressed on.

'Add the eggs,' said Delia.

'Eggs? What eggs?' I screeched. 'Since when did this recipe need eggs?'

We are blessed with long-suffering neighbours who not only are equipped with cake tins of every conceivable size but also never run out of eggs. They even believe in Acts 2:44 (holding 'everything in common'), which is jolly decent of them, especially for us.

With further generous donations from next door we succeeded in turning out a passable cake, and I was left with the washing-up while the kids disappeared into the garden because it had stopped raining.

Having cleared away in the kitchen, I went upstairs to do yet more tidying. Standing on a chair and trying to retrieve something from a high shelf in one of our cupboards, I screamed loudly as I knocked half a dozen other things to the floor. My next-door neighbour on the other side of the adjoining wall must have leapt out of her skin. Fearing the worst, she rushed straight round, thinking I might be lying helpless under a fallen bookcase.

She was at my front door before I'd even got down off the chair. She stood there, with her heart racing and her adrenaline pumping, in far greater need of first aid than I was, politely asking me if I was all right. Bless her socks!

Monday, 13 May

Living with small children is an education in itself. You'd think spelling would be my forte. It ought to be. I am an English teacher.

'How do you spell "Mars"?' Matthew asked me this evening.

'M. A. R. S.,' I replied confidently. Two minutes later he showed me the letter he had written to his friend: 'Dear Joanna, Last week we went to Grand*mars* . . .' I'm learning never to accept a question at face value.

Some subjects are harder than others: geography and theology are the worst. As the two-hour drive to Grandma's is the longest distance Matthew can imagine, how can he possibly comprehend somewhere the size of Africa? And as for God immortal, invisible and all that, he takes some explaining.

Tonight, however, we were able to sort out one detail related to our eternal destiny: namely, its location. The question arose unexpectedly while we were watching a holiday programme after tea. Following an appetising report on southern Spain, Matthew piped up with, 'When can we go to heaven?'

My puzzled parental response was at least comforting: 'When we die we'll go to heaven.'

'No, no,' he said. 'When will we go to the country Heaven?'

Blank looks all round.

'You know, with the triangles,' he added, becoming exasperated at our ignorance. 'Grandma's been there.'

'Well, that narrows it down a bit,' David remarked drily. 'Grandma's been most places besides heaven . . . yet.'

After a lot of guesswork it turned out Matthew meant Egypt, that place with the triangles . . . er . . . pyramids. I'm not quite sure how he had made the connection between heaven and Egypt, but we've ironed out this particular glitch in his theology. Egypt may have its heavenly parts but I'm sure it's not a patch on the real thing.

Tuesday, 14 May

I've been drawing on the backs of envelopes for a week. The idea of extending the house won't go away. I've worked out that a new dining room on the back and a porch on the front would give us the current dining room as a study. This thought is highly motivating. In my mind's eye I have already redesigned the room's layout, repainted the walls, put up the shelves and filled the as yet non-existent filing cabinet. The porch and new dining room don't interest me half as much. They are merely places to put things that don't belong in my study. Did I say 'my'? I meant 'our' study. I'm not really possessive about it (much).

This evening I broached the subject with David again. This time his response was a little more receptive. We had, after all, drawn up plans three years ago for a new dining room on the back but never had the money to build it. All we would have to do would be to resurrect those plans and commission a new drawing for the porch. It sounds simple. Something tells me it won't be, but anyway we've agreed to investigate the possibility.

Thursday, 16 May

Someone came to draw the plans this morning. It looks as if this idea might fly.

Monday, 20 May

I haven't cracked the waking-up routine yet; probably I never will. I need a cold flannel by the bed. A cup of tea helps. David sometimes obliges and I've recently installed a small kettle in the bedroom so I can make my own, but it feels such a long way to the dressing table from the bed at 7 a.m.

It's always harder if I've been out the night before. Last night was the first meeting of a new group from church. We are the Family Planning Group, which sounds much more entertaining than it is. In fact, it *is* fairly entertaining, as we are responsible for planning all the family services at church. Last night we planned an ambitious re-enactment of the crossing of the Red Sea; given that ours is a standard Victorian Anglican building, complete with pews, this should be interesting.

Friday, 24 May

What a panic I had yesterday. Report slips suddenly appeared in my pigeon hole at school and I was told they had to be completed by today. I sat up last night and wrote thirty in one marathon sitting. This morning I was going in to plead for an extension for the remaining thirty. I eventually tracked down my head of department, who looked rather surprised at my request.

'They're not due until the end of June,' he told me.

That's the worst thing about being part-time in a place. It's easy to get the wrong end of the stick when you are only in and out of the staffroom at odd times of the day. The person who told me they were needed by today thought I was talking about a different year group. Oh, well, at least I've done half of them already.

The man doing the drawings for the extensions came back during the week. He'd forgotten to take a few measurements. He'd said they'd be ready by the end of next week.

Saturday, 25 May

So much for the extension plans being ready. The chap drawing them rang this morning to say, sorry, his mother's house had just been sold and he couldn't do them now anyway. Between feeling resentful about anyone else's house selling when ours didn't and annoyed that we'd wasted several days with this guy, I felt thoroughly fed up. At least we hadn't paid him any money.

I've already called in architect number two.

David has been away all week again, in America on business. The last time he was away for the week all our plans for moving fell through. It's not fun having to make decisions on your own. At least this time the firm he's with allows him to call home from the office at the end of every day (that's about 10 p.m. our time). Last night I was so tired and fed up, I retreated for an early bath. As we don't have an upstairs phone, I had to spend about half an hour messing about with extension leads in order to take his call from the bath.

It worked. He was very impressed. I'm not known for my technical ability.

This week the fan oven has got the better of me. I'm supposed to knock off ten minutes for every thirty minutes required by the recipe and reduce the temperature by ten degrees, but no matter how often this formula is repeated to me, I'm defeated every time.

That's why we have a smoke alarm in the hall downstairs. This week it's worked overtime, going off like a dinner gong every evening just as I finish cooking. The children's helpful solution to this noisy problem is to open the front door. This certainly facilitates the entry of fresh air but it also acts as a warning system for the rest of the street. The sight of two small children semaphoring at the door, wafting the air in and the sound and smoke out, signals 'Tea's up at number 31'.

I console myself that it is a very sensitive alarm. I only have to boil potatoes and it goes into action. Then again I wouldn't put it past my ingenious husband to have wired it up to the grill pan, as I can't cook so much as a fish finger without it going off.

I thought yesterday that I had discovered the family-life Tip for the Week. A cure for the common early-morning row. I'd had the same row for three consecutive mornings, the one that starts 'Where's the hairbrush?' The hairbrush is one of those items, like TV remotes, that go walkabout. They are supposed to live in a fixed place but are never there when you need them. At the end of yesterday's hairbrush row I resolved at full volume (i.e., I shouted), 'I am going to buy the first hairbrush I find with a hole in the handle and I am going to attach it with string to the coat hooks in the hall.'

This I duly did and felt very smug about it.

Today I discovered the drawback. When your hairbrush has only a three-foot radius of operation, you have to bring the child to the hairbrush and not the other way round. This is not so easy as it sounds. Thus the script for early-morning rows has merely been rewritten. Now I stand in the hall with the brush and yell, 'Where's the hair?'

Monday, 27 May

Half-term again.

The second architect has rung to say he's had a nasty virus ever since we spoke to him and hasn't been able to start on our plans. He'll get round to them as soon as he can. These petty set-backs have really frustrated me. I've tried so hard to be patient and not pushy in my prayers, and I know there are so many other people putting up with far worse situations than merely working and eating in the same room, but it does get me down. There's a part of me that feels that no matter what we do, nothing will ever happen, that 'wait' might just mean 'put up with it'. The shortage of time to think about the extensions and money to build them also upsets me.

Much of David's spare time is spent sorting out the fabric and finances of the church, and it often feels as if he doesn't have much energy and interest left over for our own projects. The house issue doesn't bother him so much anyway. He's not in it all day, every day.

Why is it that all major decisions involving large sums of money get so complicated? We've tried hard to discern God's will; we've exercised 'sanctified common sense'; we're making responsible choices. And still the way forward seems full of pitfalls.

At least for this week I can concentrate on home and the children and forget about school. All I need is a little time to plan the Red Sea sermon for the family service, but I should be able to do that on Thursday when the kids are booked in for a swimming activity day at the sports centre. I don't know how many activities you can do in a swimming-pool in one day but the kids are fairly keen to go.

Thursday, 30 May

I packed the kids off for their activity day this morning. On the way there it dawned on me that this would be the first time they were going swimming without one of their parents on hand to watch them. I felt a surge of protective anxiety and almost turned round. Not even an army of attendants could watch my kids the way I do.

But I couldn't disappoint them, so instead I prolonged my departure, fussed over procedures and double-checked the staff ratios, even though I'd already asked for this information when I'd booked them in for the day. When they finally went through to the changing rooms I just about held myself back from one last hug and coaxed myself to walk away calmly.

I had to tell myself, 'This is a reasonable, responsible thing to do. I'm leaving them in the care of trained professionals . . . who have ninety-eight other children to look after as well as mine.' I couldn't quite bury my misgivings.

I should have been able to relax at home and get on with the Red Sea talk, but instead my mind fluttered from one task to another and I leapt for the phone every time it rang. Irrationality and fear are a toxic combination.

A friend of mine once defined worry as checking your nine-year-old son is safe in the bath even though he's just earned distance awards for swimming. I can identify with that. Emma is just on the verge of small forays into independence, such as going to the corner shop by herself. Already she plays out in the street on her bike with her friends, but only on the stretch of street clearly visible from the front window. Even so, I spend a ridiculous amount of time loitering in the front garden every time she's out there.

I did do a bit on the Red Sea sermon. I thought

about how frightening it must have been for the Israelites. They had to cross over in the dark, so our re-enactment won't be very accurate unless we turn the lights off. I'd imagined Moses striding out with a band of gung-ho Israelites falling in behind but it wasn't like that at all. They must have been quaking with terror. I know I would be if I had to walk across a river bed in the black of night with water banked up on either side and a terrifying army at my heels. It struck me that it doesn't really matter how they felt about the crossing at the time – the important thing was that they crossed. It comforts me that God honours our steps of obedience even when they are taken timidly.

The kids came back in one piece, tired, wrinkly and wrung out like dishcloths from their day in the pool. My fears were unfounded.

Sunday, 2 June

The Red Sea service went okay. The children who were the Red Sea waves parted bang on cue to let the Israelites through. Only the Egyptians were a bit flat: a band of little boys with drums who had been so warlike in rehearsal we'd actually asked them to tone it down a bit. We shouldn't have bothered. They were overawed by the occasion and shuffled down the aisle to the faint tapping of a solitary drum that wouldn't have scared a flock of sheep, let alone the crowd of Israelites.

The theme was 'Follow God faithfully, not fearfully'. The following bit is definitely easier when you agree with his specific recent instructions. I wish I felt more positive about work and less preoccupied with the house.

Thursday, 5 June

Happy Birthday to us! We are thirty-four today – at least I think we are. After celebrating fifteen birthdays together I tend to leave it to David to remember how old we are, but today he's not here to remind me. I think this is the first time we've celebrated our birthdays apart since we were nineteen and it feels rather strange.

When we first met there was a whole series of bizarre similarities between us, in both our background and our features. We both had short brown hair, dark eyes and square, steel-rimmed glasses. If it hadn't been for the small matter of gender, we could have been clones. We were regularly mistaken for brother and sister. The discovery that we shared the same birthday clinched the match. It didn't seem like a case of 'opposites attract', so it's been a fascinating journey over the last sixteen years finding out just how opposite we are. Letters are a good example: I'm addicted to the post and rush down in the morning to open anything addressed by hand. David, however, will put hand-written letters to one side and get round to them only after he's opened the bills. I find this behaviour incomprehensible, but never mind – at least it means I can open the crop of cards in this morning's post and leave the bills for him to enjoy later.

Friday, 6 June

David got home okay yesterday, but his suitcase was delayed. It took a diversion round Europe and turned up by taxi at 10 p.m. Good thing too. It had my present in it.

Wednesday, 12 June

This hasn't been a good week and it's only Wednesday. My state of mind has bothered me as much as anything. I've felt low and tired and fed up and haven't really had time to stop and think why I've felt this way. A mood is like a tune that you can't get out of your head, and this week's melody has been in a minor, discordant key: my classes were all rearranged, so I've had to face unfamiliar children; the man who's spent three weeks doing our extension plans has still not come up with the goods; and I have twice as many church commitments as I can handle and one less day to do it all in because the children have Friday off for teacher training. All this would be quite enough to produce the kind of mood I'm in, but for added misery we women can always rely on our hormones.

Yesterday started on a particularly harsh note. I had not slept well after a late church meeting the previous evening and I was awoken too soon after 6.30 a.m. by Matthew, who bounced into the room at full volume.

By 7.15 I had had enough of being jumped on and harangued. Matthew fires off questions at the rate of three a minute. 'Is it Tuesday?', 'How do you spell "disappear"?' and 'Will you read me a story?' represent the general tone of his enquiries. The words 'It's too early. Go away' have little or no effect unless you growl them at him, which is not only hard work in the morning but also rather unkind.

Yesterday, however, I was feeling decidedly growly so, having been dismissed rather fiercely from my room, Matthew took himself off to sulk in his bedroom. One cup of tea and several slammed cupboards later, I got round to an apology.

Today before tea I became aware that my tone of voice was very terse. In spite of my best efforts to disguise my irritation, both the kids seemed to tune in to the tense undertones in my voice. I'd tried very hard to do the right thing. While we waited for tea to be ready, we'd got out a game and sat down to have quality time together. Within minutes the children had argued over the rules and we'd all fallen out with each other.

I prayed for the patience to stay calm.

Being a parent at such moments seems too hard.

It feels as though someone has sat me in front of a piano and told me to play a masterpiece. I have neither the sheet music nor the skill, but I do have a critical audience waiting expectantly. I feel like a small child in front of a grand piano, stabbing at notes, trying hard to find a melody but only producing a meaningless noise.

The other day a friend told me how she had overheard her small son playing their piano. He was producing a dreadful racket, but she still stopped to encourage him as only a mother can. 'That's a lovely tune you're playing, dear,' she told him.

'Yes,' he replied, 'and I'm playing it in French!'

Help me, Father. On days like this I need to play my life in the key of love. You know I'm no musician, but if you sing it, I'll hum it.

Friday, 14 June

The bubble of emotion simmering inside me for the last week came to the surface and burst this morning in response to a question. Someone asked me if I missed my close friend Ruth, who moved away at the end of February.

'No, not really,' I lied and promptly burst into tears. Denial is such a powerful thing. Missing my friend has been only one thread in a whole tangled bundle of difficulties and disappointments this month, and I hadn't allowed myself to stop and think about it. My interrogator had pulled the right thread and found she'd unravelled the whole knotted mess. Thankfully she had time to stick around and help me tidy up my frayed emotions.

Talking it all through was immensely helpful. I didn't need advice, guidance or direction. All I really needed was someone to listen with understanding. People who can do this are a gift from God.

Monday, 17 June

I had a better weekend. My hormones have swung in my favour, my inner store of unexpressed emotion has been cleared out and the sun shone to boot. All the warm-weather accessories came out of the cupboard on Saturday: the sun hats and sun cream, the water pistols and the icebergs.

The icebergs were Matthew's idea. He'd asked for them last week as well but I'd been unable to decode his request. Foraging in the kitchen drawer on Saturday, he told me that he'd once swallowed an iceberg. He hadn't meant to, of course. Icebergs weren't meant to be swallowed, not whole anyway.

'What are they meant for then?' I enquired, casually.

'To keep your drink cool, silly.'

Comprehension dawned. He was looking for the ice-cube tray.

Digging it out from the back of the drawer, I

entrusted him with the task of washing and filling it. I neglected to say that one didn't wash it and fill it with the same water. Thankfully we caught him just as he was decanting the last of the dishwater into the final cube.

The water pistols were David's idea. I take the view that if you are foolish enough to supply your children with pump-action water pistols which hold several litres each and have a firing range of twenty feet, you deserve every soaking you get. So far, he's had several.

The sun hats were my idea. Buying them was the easy bit; the tricky bit is keeping them on the kids' heads while they are outside.

This morning my plan was to put as much of the Monday wash load as I could out in the sunshine. The weatherman had forecast a blazing hot day, so I'd emptied the wash basket with enthusiasm. Three machine loads later, the final set of bed linen was ready for drying. I took it out to the heavily laden rotary clothes drier which was tipped at its usual crazy angle. (It's never recovered its poise since the children used it as a fairground ride.) As I pegged up the final pillowcase, the fatigued metal pole finally gave out and the whole thing keeled over like a tree axed at its roots.

In a bid to rescue my damp washing from grass stains, I hoisted the whole contraption on to my shoulder, laundry and all. If anyone had looked over the garden wall at that point they would have seen a

'... the whole thing keeled over like a tree axed at its roots'

fully loaded rotary washing line staggering up and down the garden with no visible means of support.

I'd only just pegged it all out, so there was no way I was going to take it all in again and waste such a good drying day. But nor could I stand around doing a pole impression for several hours. I had to find some other means of supporting it. Eventually I laid it sideways across the lawn, propped at 45 degrees across a sunlounger. The effect was somewhat surreal. If Picasso had ever hung out washing, this is how he'd have done it.

My modern art dried out wonderfully. Folding it away later, I was thankful for the seasonal joys of sunny afternoons, even if they do bring out the sun hats, water pistols and icebergs.

Monday, 24 June – the blood donor

Today I gave blood.

I don't mean I worked exceptionally hard in the classroom, nor did I exert myself on the domestic front. I mean, I literally went and gave blood.

Yesterday I took the precaution of persuading a reluctant friend to come and donate with me. That way when I turned chicken overnight (which I knew I would) I'd have someone to keep me to my resolve. The plan worked. My friend took a little persuading but she eventually agreed and by this morning when my courage had failed she was firmly committed to the endeavour.

The leaflet said not to give blood on an empty stomach, so we didn't take any chances. Fortified by custard doughnuts, we arrived on time for the session. Unfortunately forty-two other people had arrived early for the session; when we saw our ticket numbers we realised despondently that our mission was doomed. We had to be back at the school gate in one hour's time and there was a twenty-five-minute queue ahead of us. I never knew blood doning was such a popular pastime.

Knowing that our noble ambitions were going to be thwarted, we made to leave. But blood donors are a generous and determined group of people. Seeing us about to depart with our full eight pints intact, the next person in the queue immediately gestured to us to go ahead of her.

With forty-two pairs of eyes boring into the back of my head, I felt a most conspicuous queue-jumper as I took my seat to answer the routine questions. I became very confused. The nurse asked me if I was married and I denied everything. A sideways glance from my companion put me back on track.

That interview turned out to be the trickiest part of the process; the rest was plain sailing. The nurse was very friendly, so my usual diversionary tactic in any nerve-racking situation (keep talking) was made easy for me. I'm not sure the other pale donors around me were appreciative of my self-conscious cheerfulness, but the nearer I got to the tea and biscuits the more jovial I became.

As I'd not given blood for a long time, the nurse told me I had to lie down for the full fifteen minutes afterwards. I had no objections but was very amused that she wrote the time I was allowed up on a Post-it note and stuck it on my tummy. I'll have to try that one at home next time I flake out on the sofa.

I've worn my 'Be nice to me. I've given blood today' sticker prominently all day, hoping to extract maximum sympathy from my husband and off-spring. They were unimpressed.

Only Matthew was curious. Ages ago he'd come with me to the hospital when I had to give a blood sample. He'd been fascinated. I'd explained to him that it was to help the doctor decide how to make Mummy feel better.

He'd immediately volunteered to be drained of *all* his blood. 'Then there won't be any left to come out if I fall over, and I don't like it coming out,' he declared.

This time I explained that Mummy's blood would be given to help other people who were poorly. He seemed to accept this explanation, although why anyone should want any more of such 'yucky stuff' was beyond him.

David kept stoically silent throughout this conver-sation. Nothing will ever induce him to repeat the experience he'd had when, as a student, he'd been dragged along to the blood bank (against his better judgment) in a macho huddle of mates from college.

It really wasn't a wise move for someone with such

a nervous disposition towards needles. He survived okay till the nurse asked him if he *was* okay. It was her tone of voice that unnerved him. It sounded like the kind of question you ask someone who is fast fading away, so he promptly complied with her expectations and, much to the amusement of his mates, his bed became a hive of medical activity, with nurses flapping flipcharts in his face and raising his legs in the air.

He recovered consciousness, if not his dignity, and made it to the tea-and-biscuits table, where a well-meaning volunteer looked at him with concern and said, 'Are you okay?'

That put him back on the couch for another half-hour, by which time his friends had even given up heckling through the window.

I suppose now I've signed up I shall receive a regular reminder in the post. I've been given a little cardboard book which gets stamped every visit. It's meant to motivate me to go for a championship record of donation. Clearly a casual one-off isn't enough to sustain the service.

You could say that about a lot of things in life, really: marriage, bringing up kids, worthwhile occupations. They all take effort to pursue. Perhaps what I need to encourage me is a little book that clocks up my commitment or records my perseverance – the buckets of effort, the fathoms of faithfulness and, let's face it, even the litres of tears. Come to think of it, I think there is a record being kept somewhere by someone.

Friday, 28 June

The children brought their school reports home with them this afternoon. I put them to one side to read together after tea. Emma couldn't wait to hear what the envelope contained and hung on every shade and nuance of the teacher's opinion. Matthew, on the other hand, was sublimely indifferent. I didn't know whether to congratulate him on having the self-confidence not to care or to chide him for his lack of interest. Given that his report was good, I didn't do either. We allowed them both to bask in the sunshine of our warm approval and celebrated with jam doughnuts.

If Matthew is still worrying about school, he doesn't show it. I'll have the chance to speak to his teacher next week at parents' evening.

Monday, 1 July

Another Monday, but the end is in sight. Only two more Monday mornings to go before the end of term, and July is stuffed full of distractions so the time will fly.

Wednesday, 3 July

It was the children's parents' evening this evening. David and I really look forward to this event and always make an effort to go together. It's not just that we hope to hear good things about our children but the entertainment factor is also fairly high. The news books are the best bit – children are opinionated reporters of daily life. In my own school news book I once recorded the fact that my mother was 'small, fat and happpy'. This libellous description had been left open on display for all the other parents to read, and just in case anyone should still fail to recognise her, I'd also drawn a smiling fat lady on stick legs.

My own children had not embarrassed us in the same way until this evening. We set out in good time, leaving the children with a neighbour. We had strict instructions from Emma as to where to see her artwork on the walls, but we knew that on our return we would be quizzed on the one picture we'd somehow fail to spot.

Looking at the displays and reading the news books at least gives you something to do while you are waiting to see the teacher. When it gets to our turn I can't help feeling intimidated. Maybe it's the fact of sitting on a little school chair with my knees up to my chest and my chin only just higher than the teacher's desk – I don't know what it is but suddenly I have a job remembering that I am a parent and not a pupil. Two minutes in front of the impressive Mrs S. and I revert to model-pupil mode. I nod obediently and sit up straight. I have to fight the urge to raise my hand before asking questions.

This evening I also had to fight the urge to give

an account of myself as a mother, having just read my children's news books. Emma's had featured an account of our stay at Butlin's for the Spring Harvest Easter Event. According to Emma's report, the highlight of the whole holiday was the evening we offered hospitality to the rest of our party; she recorded the fact that 'One night there was fifteen people in our coffin.'

An inept attempt at the word 'chalet'? Or a comment on the standard of budget accommodation? Either way one wonders what the teacher thought of it. It sounded more like an undertakers' convention than a Christian holiday.

Next came Matthew's description of his whoopee cushion: what he does with it, what noise it makes, complete with illustration. This crowned our humiliation. Defenceless parents ought to have the right of denial.

Knowing now how my mother felt, and aware that this is thirty years too late, I shall now come clean: 'My mother is small. She is happy.'

Friday 6 July

My prayers this week have mostly been petitions. Among other things, I have been preoccupied with daily-bread issues about how we are going to afford the extensions if they go ahead. This morning in my Bible reading I read 2 Corinthians 9:10: 'Now he who supplies seed to the sower and bread for food will also supply and *increase* [my italics] your store of seed and will enlarge the harvest of your righteousness.' I was so taken with this promise of God's provision that I decided to commit it to memory. It was a beautiful morning and I wanted to go out for a run, so in between finding my trainers and pulling on my kit I scribbled the verse down on some paper. Before I left I invited God to come along with me and talk to me some more about this verse.

I run two or three times a week if I can. It keeps me sane. It doesn't make me super-fit, but at least I can eat custard doughnuts without a bad conscience.

The solitude of the country lane this morning was ideal for Scripture memorisation. I like to say the verse aloud and do some actions as well – it's the Sunday-school teacher in me. So there I was, happily jogging along, waving my arms about and talking to myself about seed stores and harvests, when I was reminded of the one ingredient necessary for a harvest that I had overlooked: rain.

'Yes, very funny, Lord. I take the point. Please could it stop raining now?' I'd passed the half-way point, so there was little point in turning round. If it carried on raining, I'd get soaked.

It did and I did.

Within minutes I found myself running through a downpour. It wasn't cold, so I didn't mind that much to start off with. I jogged along, reminding myself of the biblical connections between rain and blessing (leaving Noah out of it, of course). The verse had gone soggy in my hand and I threw it away, feeling more certain than ever that God had brought it to my attention to encourage me.

And then it thundered. I sobered up pretty quickly and realised that running through an open field in the middle of a thunderstorm was perhaps not a very clever thing to be doing. I may be only five foot six, but I was the tallest object for hundreds of yards in every direction. I wondered if the soles of my trainers were made of rubber and whether that would make any difference. I increased my speed considerably.

Twenty minutes later, and soaked to the skin, I reached home safely. It was still raining and my trainers squelched on the pavement as I came down our road. The whole episode had been rather exhilarating. There was I, pleading for God's blessing, and he had shown me that he can and will bless abundantly but that I cannot dictate a convenient time for his blessing to arrive. Nor should I lose sight of God's awesome power. Were it not for the fact that he chooses graciously to bless me, he could sweep me away in a moment.

Joy needs to be tempered with respect and praise mingled with awe.

Saturday, 6 July

We saw the first of three builders today. In spite

of my worries about cash we are at least going to get some estimates. The architect has also finally returned our plans and submitted an application for planning permission.

Tuesday, 9 July – life is a sandwich

This week is about as crammed as it's possible for a week to be. Not only am I still teaching but I've also agreed to do a first-aid course for two evenings after school. My readership training course has started, so that takes another evening, Emma has a school concert and a school assembly at which my presence is required and Ruth is coming to stay with her two children overnight on Friday. To cap it all, David is away for a day and a night this week, which gets him neatly out of attendance at concerts or assemblies.

Life at the moment feels like the stuffed salad sandwich I had for my lunch today. Too many tastes and textures, too much crammed in. On the plate it looks appetising but take one bite and you end up with mayonnaise down your chin and tomato slices in your lap. My overloaded schedule functions just like my overloaded sandwich: as I push something in at one side, something else falls out the other.

I used to think I had life neatly arranged. The layers that jostle for space in my schedule/sandwich are: motherhood, the foundational layer that flavours everything I do; marriage, the tasty main feature; finally, a tossed salad of teaching and writing, sprinkled with a bracing dash of public speaking (the element of terror that adds relish to life).

Out of all these ingredients teaching had been my gherkin experience this year (anyone who picks the gherkins out of McDonald's burgers will know what I mean). Now that I am considering dropping this ingredient from my sandwich I have struggled with a sense of failure. 'Other women manage this,' I've said to myself, and 'Schools need Christian teachers,' or even 'I trained to do this.' But I think I have finally decided that this particular ingredient doesn't blend with the rest of my sandwich.

Life's too short to stick stubbornly at tasks you feel you ought to do if you don't have to do them. I realise I'm very privileged to be able to make this choice. For many women the paid-employment ingredient is not a choice but a necessity, the majority of them deciding to work part-time. It strikes me that this only adds to the stuffed salad sandwich effect we women feel. We have so many fillings to choose from: the motherhood filling, with all its variant flavours of nursemaid, playmate, educator, taxi-driver and counsellor. Then there's the housekeeper filling: chief cook, domestic engineer, gardener and home decorator.

These two fillings have kept my sandwich well stuffed for at least the first five years of motherhood, but now yet more options offer themselves to me. I could volunteer to hear children read at school, join the PTA, run a toddler group . . . I could do all of these things and take up part-time employment if I was really keen (or crazy, depending how you look at it).

In the middle of all this activity, there are also relationships to be maintained: I am someone's wife; I am someone else's daughter (help! it's her birthday tomorrow); and I have friends with whom I'd like to exchange more than the annual sentence on the Christmas card. All this seems like an uphill task, given my crowded diary. But because I really do seem to be aiming for superwoman status, I must somehow squeeze in those essential elements of modern motherhood: personal grooming, physical exercise and spiritual nourishment.

And I wonder why I'm feeling so exhausted.

I think I should take to eating a simpler sandwich. This one's giving me indigestion.

Thursday, 11 July

Yesterday I had one free hour in which to dash into town. Not only did I have my mother's belated birthday gift to sort out but also David had asked me to cash in his penny collection. He'd promised me a meal out on it next week. With this tasty prospect in view I patiently counted pennies in the bank for twenty minutes and reached the grand total of £10.50. Calculating that this wasn't going to get us much further than Tesco's café, I decided it wasn't even worth bagging up. Disheartened, I shovelled it all back into the bottom of my shopping bag.

Having got my mother's gift and fast running out of time, my final task was to whizz round a cheap hardware shop, one of those places where you always see at least five other items that you suddenly realise you need in spite of the fact that you didn't know you needed them until you saw them.

Thus I arrived at the check-out with a loaded basket and opened my bag to pay. I was intending to pay by cheque but to my horror I couldn't find my cheque card. Then I remembered leaving it beside the phone at home in the morning.

For a moment I debated paying with the pennies from David's collection but decided against it: shopping in a discount store is bad enough for one's street cred – paying in pennies would have been beyond the pale!

When I admitted that I was only flush with embarrassment, not cash, the check-out girl was very nice about it. She offered to put all the shopping back on the shelves for me. I came home mentally exhausted and emotionally overhauled. I'd achieved nothing.

Some days you wonder why you bother.

Friday, 12 July

I've made it to Friday. I didn't make it to the school assembly but that was the only casualty out of all this week's commitments. Ruth arrived safely and

David returned on time. We had just settled down for a chat after getting the kids to bed when David delivered us tea on a tray and some startling news.

Today he was offered a job, a good job at that. I could tell he was excited and, in spite of my stunned feelings, I didn't want to deflate him. After all, it's not every day you get offered a job you haven't applied for. There was just one teeny little technical problem about this job: it's not here. It's 150 miles away, in Lancashire.

My confusions and questions tumbled out all at the same time. What kind of job? When would it start? Where would we live? We can't move the kids. What about me? What about the extensions? And so on and so on. The presence of a close friend to sit in on this conversation proved a blessing, expecially a close friend who had so recently re-located herself.

As to the details, there weren't many. The job was as vague as the offer, and the person who had made it wouldn't be able to firm it up for three or four months, if at all. We didn't know quite what to make of it. Is this the direction for which we'd been told to wait or is it a red herring to distract us? How should we respond? We are on the verge of extending the house. Should we wait again?

Sunday, 14 July

My readings for the week ahead are all from Job.

I can't help feeling depressed about this. There he was, good old Job, a faithful follower of God who had everything going for him. Then, *whoosh*, he loses it all in one weekend. What are you saying, Lord? Here I am, on the brink of achieving a minor goal (getting a study), about to start two years of readership training, heavily involved with church activities: am I to give it all up? I feel a bit aggrieved about this job offer. Yes, I can see that David would have a lot to gain, but what about me? What about the kids?

The Bible reading notes remind me that 'God is the scriptwriter.' Okay, God, this is your play, not mine.

Monday, 15 July

Today was the highlight of the children's sporting calendar: the annual school sports day. Following hard on the heels of the Olympics this year, this is the one event I wouldn't miss for the world.

They have been training hard: yesterday Emma told me that the higher she lifted her knees, the faster she went. This I have to see. Sports day is two hours spent sitting with friends in the baking heat (if we are lucky), squinting into the sunshine, waiting to shout ourselves silly for the entire duration of our children's three-minute appearance.

For the children, the audience matters far more than the competition. They love being able to nudge a friend and say, 'There's my mum. She's wearing a silly hat,' or 'There's Dad with a camera.' Dads with cameras are par for the course, it's the dads with stopwatches you want to watch out for.

At our school, everyone's a winner. The last child over the line gets as big a cheer as the first, and anyone who stumbles is immediately set back on their feet by the sound of several hundred mummies saying, 'Ahh,' simultaneously.

When all the racing, jumping and skipping events have been completed by the children, it's our turn to take part with as much dignity as we can muster. Last year I ran in the mothers' race, only because my children would never have forgiven me if I hadn't. It wasn't very serious. Most of us ran in bare feet, having kicked off unsuitable sandals at the last moment. We were all very sheepish at the starting line but as soon as the gun went off, three or four keenies from the back of the pack (all wearing trainers) shot forward, making the rest of us look as if we were out for a Sunday stroll.

It's usually the dads who get competitive. The fathers' race is a jostling of egos – they take it all rather seriously. What most of them don't know is that when the starting pistol cracks the two ladies holding the finishing line will also set off at a run down the field and by the time the men have reached the line, they'll have run twice the distance they expected.

And for the finale: the toddlers' race. Thirty-five

'And for the finale...'

three-year-olds are deposited on one side of the starting line by their mummies, who then go to the other side of the finishing line. On the command 'Go' all the mummies shout for their little darlings and about five chubby-legged children will set off in the desired direction. Confused by the cacophony of names, twenty more will wander off in differing directions and the remaining ten stay put and sob for their mothers, who appear to be trapped behind a rope twenty-five yards away.

Entertaining? It beats the Olympics any day.

Wednesday, 17 July

This evening Emma filled me in on her mathematical progress. 'I know what a dot with a line under it with another dot below that means,' she said, self-importantly.

'Really?' I said, sounding impressed but struggling to visualise the mathematical symbol she'd described.

Before I'd worked it out, she offered me her definition. 'It means sharing, Mummy. If you have eight sweets and share them between four friends they get two each.'

Having had the word 'division' on the tip of my tongue, her definition surprised me for a moment or two. Then it dawned on me that the outcome of sharing or dividing is always the same. It's only the attitude that differs.

Listening to the news tonight, I thought what a difference such a change in attitude would make in some of the world's troubled places. What a shame it is that we adults have dropped the friendly word 'share' in preference for the more clinical 'divide'.

Thursday, 18 July

This morning it was Matthew's mathematical insights that kept us amused. He was practising his ordinal numbers. He used to have a problem with these: 'First' was easy to remember but it was usually followed up by 'toothed' and 'threef', instead of 'second' and 'third'.

Now, however, someone has taught him a witty little jingle to help him remember. (It probably came in helpful on sports day.) He used it this morning to count us as we each got dressed.

It started with 'Zero, the hero' (an alarming post-modernist concept for a playground rhyme, I thought to myself). Daddy, first into his tie and shirt, qualified for this position. Next came Emma, who was announced to be 'first the worst' by her brother, who then rushed off to get dressed himself. This put him, conveniently, in second place. 'Second the best,' he proclaimed, yanking on the last item of clothing.

This left yours truly, the only family member still slouching around in a dressing-gown at twenty past eight. 'What will I be when I get dressed then?' I enquired.

He could barely stifle his mirth: 'Third, the one with the hairy chest!'

I wish I hadn't asked.

Friday, 19 July

I've done it! I've got to the end of term. I've taught my last lesson, marked my last set of homework, completed my final register, returned all the books, tidied out my drawer and bid everyone a joyful farewell. Yippee!

I am elated not just by the prospect of the long summer holiday but also by the knowledge that I am not going back in September. At Easter I said to God that I would continue teaching if he put me in a part-time post as clearly as he had put me in this one. I am very relieved that he hasn't.

Having worked through the guilt and failure aspects of this choice (we need the money), I am now relishing the pleasant prospect of arranging my own timetable. Most of what I want to do revolves around my computer at home, and the joy of shouting at a computer is that it doesn't shout back, unlike teenagers. These pursuits are likely to be less lucrative, but I feel incredibly privileged to be able to do what I love to do rather than what I have to do, and I am delighted to have had returned to me that portion of my mind and my diary that was given over to teaching.

The saga of the extensions rumbles on. Should we build or will we move next year? David's possible job offer has also complicated our forward planning. At times like this life feels like a journey without a map. No, that's not quite right. There is a map and God is reading it; he just won't let us peep over his shoulder.

Now that he's had a week to think about the offer, David feels that it was rather vague. He's been doing some work for the firm for some time while in his current job, and perhaps all that was really meant was 'If you were thinking of changing jobs, talk to us first,' which is quite a long way from 'We'd like to offer you a job.' All the same his Bible readings have been all about not rejecting opportunities that come out of the blue, so we can't dismiss the whole idea.

Meanwhile the thought of another winter in our cramped conditions appals me, so what's to be done?

Over and over again I have to remind myself that I cannot dictate my preferences about this journey to God. He gives us one direction at a time and we are simply supposed to follow it. My frustration with all this uncertainty occasionally boils over but I have to believe he will show us the right way at the right time.

For now, with term behind me, I feel so relieved, as if the rest of my life beckons – but who knows where to?

Monday, 22 July

Monday again and this is birthday week, our summer equivalent of Christmas minus the tree. Around here birthdays are like buses; we wait for ages and then they all come at once. The children's are separated by a mere six days.

Their birthdays would not have fallen in the same week had they complied with my timetable, but as one arrived late and the other early, the result is that we swing into party mode for one week each summer. Party mode for them, that is; headless-chicken mode for me.

Every year I vow, 'This'll be the last party. Next year we're having an outing,' and this is the first year I have fulfilled that vow, at least for one of them. On Saturday I took Emma and three friends to the cinema. It was a boiling-hot day, so I spent a happy hour and half sitting back in the air-conditioned auditorium thoroughly enjoying the fact that I was not passing the parcel, pinning the tail or pouring the lemonade. It wasn't quite hassle-free. They still all came back for a birthday tea, complete with cake. I did a swimming-pool cake, which is a great idea for non-cooks like me whose cakes always sink. You just fill the dip in the middle with chopped up jelly and call it a pool. It was a breeze.

Matthew has not been so easily persuaded out of a party, so this Friday, at four o'clock, I face the prospect of seven five-year-olds for two hours.

Memories of previous parties don't console me. Small boys eat vast quantities of anything sweet and spurn sensible sandwiches. Their enthusiasm for games lasts only for as long as it takes you to explain the rules, and their primary entertainment is to charge *en masse* from one end of the house to the other like a herd of wildebeest. I feel exhausted already. I understand why so many other parents take the burger-bar option.

He is very excited. He told the toy-shop lady today that he would be five on Friday and that the toy we were buying was for the 'pasta parcel'. His cake will be a swamp landscape: rivers of lime jelly interspersed with sand dunes of brown sugar and decorated with his favourite plastic monster pets.

We closed Emma's birthday with a bedtime prayer thanking God for the day she came into our lives. As I peeked in later and saw her curled up contentedly with all her new toys and trappings around the room, the expense and the effort were swallowed up by an overwhelming sense of privilege.

Father, it might help me to remind me about that sense of privilege on Friday . . . any time around four.

Saturday, 27 July

I survived the herd of wildebeest. Matthew thought it was a great party, which was a relief to all. Today we came down to Mum's. Emma has been delivered to camp for the first time ever. She has a friend to go with and seemed very excited at the prospect. I took them over this afternoon, complete with all their kit, sleeping bags, torches, midnight-feast treats, etc. Fleecy was conspicuously absent. She has slept with Fleecy since she was one week old, but last night she decided bravely that camp was not the best place for a full-size sheepskin comforter. She took a small teddy instead.

The campsite is in an idyllic setting in Kent – a big field with a wood, a stream and a log cabin. It's not very far from Mum's, so Matthew and I are going to stay here for the week. He is too young to go to camp and I have promised to make it up to him by camping out for one night with him in a tent I have borrowed from a friend.

David and I agreed before I came away that we would once again set aside a week to pray specifically for God to show us what to do about the extensions. As we will be apart all week, this will give us time to mull things over and we'll pool our conclusions at the end of the week.

Monday, 29 July

I went to church yesterday morning with my ears pinned back, hoping that God would say something dramatic. He didn't. The service was all about marriage and I was challenged about the confrontational attitude I sometimes take towards David. When it comes to housing hassles I have often made him uncomfortably aware of my opinions and preferences. With a singular lack of anything else to report I thought I may as well pass this thought on to David when he rang last night.

'I think I should follow whatever direction the Lord gives you,' I said. (This was a brave offer from someone so set on extending to someone so cautious about spending.)

'That's interesting,' he said, pleasantly surprised. He then gave me a verse that he'd read that morning, all about not being afraid but carrying out plans with courage. He took this to mean we should go ahead, but we still thought we'd keep an open mind till the end of the week.

This morning I picked up a book and read a quote from Martin Luther, who seems to have had quite a lot to say to me this year one way and another. The words struck me with such force I wrote them down.

'This is the glory of Faith, simply not to know: not to know where you are going, not to know what you are doing, not to know what you must suffer . . . and captive to follow the naked voice of God.' This quotation was followed by the comment: 'Faith goes forward, whatever the outlook.'

Wednesday, 31 July

I pitched our borrowed tent on Mum's lawn at 5

p. m. last night. Matthew was very excited. We sat down to supper and by the time we got up, it was raining. The one evening we choose to sleep outside it had to rain. The tent hadn't leaked, so we risked it. In fact, we had quite a comfortable night, and it did me good to go to bed at least three hours earlier than normal, even if we did wake with the dawn. I hope Emma stayed dry at camp.

Thursday, 1 August

David rang again tonight and again we discussed our decision about the extensions. Neither of us felt as certain as we'd like to feel. Perhaps in asking for a clear answer we were expecting too much – after all, it's a fairly petty personal dilemma. On a global scale God has far bigger concerns. We both felt a bit flat.

Friday, 2 August

David rang again. Today he had a surprise call from the only builder who'd given us a decent quote, the one we would employ if only we were sure it was the right thing to do. The builder said that he'd had a cancellation from someone whose extension he'd been about to start and so, if we liked his quote, he could start our job at the end of next week, three months earlier than he had expected to be available. Would we like him to do the job? David took this turn of events to be the green light we'd been looking for and immediately said yes. Decisive action from someone who hasn't yet organised the finance or received the planning permission, but at least we feel we've had the divine go-ahead.

Saturday, 3 August

I picked Emma up from camp this morning and came home. She was very grubby and very happy, having spent the whole week outdoors, swinging through trees, wading through streams and sleeping round camp fires. She didn't stop talking all the way home. She hadn't been homesick once and had about her an air of confidence obviously acquired from her week away. The best bit had been something called 'survival': they were given one match, a tin of beans, a packet of sausages and a bag of marshmallows and sent off to survive in the woods. They built a den, started a fire and roasted the marshmallows. She was well impressed.

I think she was asleep within minutes of being tucked up in her own bed and reunited with Fleecy.

Wednesday, 7 August

The builders arrive tomorrow and we still haven't received the planning permission. The town council told me yesterday that the papers would be signed at the end of the day, and I asked them to keep them in the office so that I could personally collect them today. Today when I rang up to check, the papers had been signed and put in the post.

Thursday, 8 August

The postman brought the planning permission at seven thirty this morning and the builders arrived at eight! By ten, I had got the hang of making a gallon of strong, sweet tea on the hour, every hour. I've arranged for the children to be out with friends all day today while we get used to having our home overrun by builders.

Friday, 9 August

Today they started digging the foundations. The children spent most of the day hanging out of the back door, fascinated by all that was going on. Our small lawn is rapidly disappearing under a pile of building materials. Thankfully we only have to put up with a week of this before we go away on holiday and leave them to it.

Friday, 16 August – of holiday memories

The whole week has been one mad rush of pre-holiday preparation. The milk's been cancelled, the cases have come down from the loft, and all our decent clothes are stacked in piles, ready to be packed. I've shopped, made tea, washed clothes, made tea, talked to the bank, made tea, talked to Ken the builder, made tea, packed, made tea, and so on and so on.

Mind you, I haven't been the only one working hard. In one week the builders have dug the foundations and finished the walls. They are ready to start the roof tomorrow. Today I left detailed instructions about light fittings, sockets, and switches, plastering and flooring, all of which we hope will be done by the time we return. I also handed over keys and arranged for a neighbour to drop in from time to time. The lads will need to make their own tea from now on, so I've left out the big teapot and six sturdy mugs and bought three bags of sugar.

Several friends have been fairly horrified that we are planning to go away and leave our home to be rearranged in our absence but I think it's the best way. Building sites and children don't mix. We've already had to mount a rescue operation for several frogs Matthew spotted trapped in a trench that was about to be filled with concrete.

I feel it's all worked out wonderfully. Only the bank is dragging its heels a bit. But we signed the forms this week and they've promised us the funds will be ready when we come back.

Sitting on a beach in the South of France has to be the ultimate way to survive having an extension done to your home, and I'm really looking forward to it. We went to the South of France a few years ago, when the children were only one and three respectively. We drove all the way to Provence and vowed, 'Never again,' when we arrived. Somewhere near Dijon I remember getting out of the car and refusing to get back in. Irrationally, I pleaded to be allowed to walk. It was that bad.

The year after that we went to France again but not so far this time. We spent two weeks in Brittany. Then we had several British holidays, and now we have once again been tempted by the long haul to the sun, but we are not going to drive. Tomorrow we catch the boat to Spain via the Bay of Biscay. I've already packed the travel pills. I hope it will all be worth it.

We are staying in a caravan and I'm hoping this will give us a taste of the French way of life without having to experience the French wildlife. On that first camping holiday in Provence several hundred slugs held a nightly convention on our groundsheet. This would not have mattered so much if I had not had to get up regularly to settle Matthew, who was still a baby. Padding across the tent in the dark was apt to be a squelchy experience.

At least slugs stay on the ground. Caterpillars climb. I know this from experience. On that same holiday I woke one night with the certain sensation that a careless caterpillar had fallen from the roof of our tent, landed safely on my neck and slid down my back. I had been soundly asleep but my

'David awoke to a vision....'

reactions were instantaneous: scrabbling for a torch and stripping off my night attire, I stood on the bed and shrieked for all I was worth. Assaulted out of his slumber by a flying pillow, David awoke to a vision of his demented spouse standing precariously on the bed, peeling off her pyjamas and shouting, 'Get it off me!' Seen from outside, I guess this silhouetted scenario would have been highly entertaining.

To his credit, David's response was swift and efficient. He found and expelled the hairy beast, or at least what was left of it, and then had to spend several more minutes patiently persuading me back into my shaken-out sleeping bag.

'All things bright and beautiful,' I can sing with conviction. It's in the line that follows it that I falter . . .

If the grubs and slugs of Provence were hard to put up with, the flora and fauna of Brittany held further delights for us the following year when we booked a caravan instead of a tent. Admittedly it was a fairly low-budget caravan (my bed was supported at one end by an upturned bucket), but at least we felt a few feet removed from the creepy-crawlies.

Lulled into this false sense of security, I allowed myself a lie-in one morning while David took the children to fetch breakfast.

While I slumbered two little sparrows followed a trail of crumbs through the open awning and into the caravan. They hopped on to the previous night's supper table and helped themselves to a feast of crumbs.

Waking to the sound of fluttering is not a pleasant experience for someone with a nervous disposition towards birds. (I find small birds in confined places ten times more terrifying than slugs and grubs.) David and the children returned to find me cowering and whimpering at the bottom of my sleeping bag while the two startled sparrows flew sorties from one end of the van to the other.

I know such fears are irrational. I also know that I should not show such a selective appreciation of God's wonderful creation. My children make up for my shortcomings in this department. Matthew in particular has a passion for small creatures. He used not to like them. I remember him screaming, 'Dye it, Mummy, dye it,' at any passing spider – not a request to alter the insect's natural colour chemically, rather a demand that I terminate its existence. The discovery of ladybirds was the turning point for him. He adores them. We have to stop and admire every one we find. His interest has now widened to all small creatures: he tells me that he 'necorises' (recognises) particular snails in our garden and he even strokes the frogs in our pond, much to his sister's fascinated disgust.

I feel that his enthusiasm more than makes up for my inadequate appreciation of creepy-crawlies. So long as he doesn't want a wormery in his bedroom or to keep toads in the bath, I shall encourage him whole-heartedly . . . from a safe distance.

Tuesday, 20 August

We arrived on the campsite today after two very successful nights on the ferry and a day and half in Spain. We took the scenic route through the Pyrenees, which was . . . well, scenic really, but also fairly nauseating in terms of hairpin bends. The children had had enough of the journey by that stage and asked, 'Are we nearly there yet?' every five minutes.

The site, van and location all seem very agreeable, much to my surprise. I've been in a fairly pessimistic frame of mind and have found it hard not to worry. The fact that we have arrived at all astounds me. On the boat I worried that the children would fall overboard or the boat would capsize. In Spain I worried that we would get lost, run out of petrol or not find our hotel. None of these things happened.

I keep telling myself not to spoil the gifts of life, health and holidays by worrying, but I just can't seem to help it. Such a long way from home, handling strange currency, eating strange food – it's all very unsettling. I try hard not to show my anxiety to the kids but Emma is very sensitive to any cause for concern. On Monday night we stayed in a monastery hostel and had a very Spanish meal, served late in the evening. It had been a really hot day, and while we were eating a storm broke with a dramatic crash of thunder and a downpour of rain. Emma looked anxiously at us. Would the building be washed away? she wondered.

David, who's not always as patient as he could be with irrational fears, said, 'Yes, it probably will. Having stood for several hundred years, it is now very likely that a shower of rain will wash it down the hillside; probably at this very moment all the monks are legging it down the drive as fast as they can, dodging the rain and falling masonry.'

We all laughed and saw the funny side of it – and then the lights went out! Poor Emma, even though they came back on in minutes, it was clear she'd had a fright. This evening there was another thunderstorm just after we'd got the kids to bed. Emma bounced out of bed with the first crash: 'Will the van leak?' 'Will the lightning hit the trees?' 'Will we be washed away?' This time we took a calm 'Mummy and Daddy are in charge here' tone of voice and settled her back down. The storm rumbled on all evening and, I have to admit, it does sound terrifying when you're in a caravan.

Saturday, 31 August

We've all had to get used to storms. We've had several. The worst one began at three this morning with a crash of thunder so loud I sat bolt-upright with premonitions of Judgment Day, having been sound asleep a moment before. It was followed by a buzzing from the local electricity sub-station and the power went off. Five minutes later the rain arrived. We have woken every morning (and quite a few nights) to the sound of rain drumming on the caravan roof. It is not a soothing noise. It is a noise I never want to hear again. We go home in two days' time now, and if there were an earlier ferry we'd be on it. We seem to have been in the one location where the clouds empty their Atlantic loads of rain before dispersing over the Pyrenees. It has rained and rained and rained.

We've tried to make the best of it, but by the time we'd visited the local aquarium and taken the kids white-water rafting, we'd had enough of water and were begging, 'Could we have some sunshine now, please?'

After five days of rain I was going crazy and suggested that we drive the hundred miles back through the mountains into Spain. We set off early and didn't stop till the sun came out, which happened to be in Pamplona, where we had a very happy day, not returning until the sun went down. After that day the weather seemed to improve a little.

We picked a reasonable day for the activity David was most looking forward to: going up a mountain by steam train and walking back down. Everyone else seemed to have the same idea for that day, so when we arrived at the little station there were long

priest. I thought of my fears and anxieties during the long journey here. 'We are fickle creatures, happy when the sun shines and depressed when it doesn't.' Too true, I thought. 'Life is like a steep climb up a mountain, often hard going but think of the view.' I thought of the views we'd enjoyed on our mountain climb.

I was sorry when the service ended. It was so full of sunshine and love. God's smiling presence seemed tangible and I felt I was being gently teased for all my uptight anxiety. Back at the start of the holiday, in the monastery, I'd bought a new bookmark on which were the words of a lovely Spanish proverb: 'Always look ahead. Smile at life. Serve love.' Good words to take home from the peace of this morning.

Tuesday, 3 September

We reached home at seven o'clock this evening. After a two-day journey we felt a sudden surge of excitement as we neared our newly extended house. Emma covered her eyes. What would it look like? Would it be finished? Would it still be a building site?

It's a strange experience, coming home to find your front door somewhere other than where you left it, but thankfully the key still worked. Holding our breath in nervous anticipation, we gave the place its first inspection. We needn't have worried; it was all virtually finished and looked better than we'd hoped. The new downstairs loo flushed; the lights worked; and all the doors opened and closed. Like excited children, we had to try it all out.

Admittedly there was a layer of red dust over every surface throughout the whole house (apart from the kitchen) and some furniture had been rearranged, but apart from that you'd never have known that there had been workmen crawling all over the place. Some wonderful person had been in to clean the kitchen, so we could fix up some supper straight away.

After unloading the car, I couldn't face unpacking. The children return to school tomorrow and it was the most I could do to find clean uniforms and PE bags.

Thursday, 5 September

Two days back from holiday and ten wash loads later, the dining room is still strewn with piles of laundry waiting to be ironed and I'm feeling like I need another holiday. Ken the builder came round yesterday to arrange to do the few remaining jobs. I wish I could have been more than simply appreciative of all his hard work, but as the bank hasn't processed the finances we still can't pay him. Thankfully he doesn't seem too worried about this.

Saturday, 7 September

Yesterday I cleared the dining room of ironing and

today we began to turn it into a study. The table was shifted out into the extension, where we shall eat from now on. So what if the floor is concrete and the walls are bare plaster?

I've yet to buy a desk and a filing cabinet and I shall need some shelves. Today I contented myself by tidying the bookcase and putting a wall planner on the wall.

Monday, 9 September – of navy knickers and name tapes

I wasn't very prepared for the autumn term this year. Returning from holiday, as we did, one day before it started meant it came as a shock. It has taken me most of the weekend to catch up with myself and sort out the children's winter uniforms.

Mention the word 'autumn' and you get a variety of responses, depending on who you speak to: 'golden leaves and misty evenings' from a romantic, 'harvest baskets of apples and marrows' from a gardener, and 'navy knickers and name tapes' from a mother.

Having weathered several Septembers with children at school, I have developed certain opinions about, and aversions to, this back-to-school season. For shopkeepers the season begins in mid-June, which is when they sell sensible winter trousers and pinafores, woolly tights and thick socks. Heaven help you if you go looking for any of these items during the last week in August. If you want to be prepared for September, you must purchase clothes a size too big three months early and hope for a summer growth spurt. Leave your shopping till late August and all you will find are a few samples of whatever you need, in the wrong size, and the girl on the till will shake her head in disbelief when you enquire, 'Will you be getting any more in?' I ask you: who needs to buy long grey trousers in September? Only half the mothers in the country.

The first of my late-August chores is to find the PE kit bags. These came home back in July. Considering the build-up of twelve bi-weekly sessions of sweaty exercise in the same kit, the bags ought to have walked home by themselves. Once located, I have to check over and disinfect the contents.

The next task is to ensure that everyone is still wearing pumps that fit them. If not, it's time to shunt all the pairs down the sibling order and buy a new pair for whoever has the biggest feet.

Having done this, we get to the really tedious bit: the 'naming of parts'. Well, labelling them, to be more precise. 'Everything must be named,' declared the reception teacher when we first went along for our preparation visits to school. Helping a reception class get dressed after PE made me understand why teachers are so insistent on this point. But labelling the kit is still an unbearably tedious job.

I have sewed on name tapes, embroidered initials, ironed on labels and simply written on care labels in

Biro when I've been in a hurry. Whichever option I go for, I can guarantee that after the first four shirts/skirts I'm bored out of my mind, and when I get to the socks I toss them aside recklessly. Buying a replacement pair of socks seems a far more attractive option than sewing on any more labels.

Mind you, if you are going to sew on labels, you need to think ahead because these also need to be ordered well in advance of that last dreadful week in August. In fact, the only task that really has to be done in the final week is the school-shoes shopping trip. I tried to get out of this last year. Matthew's sandals still fitted him fine, so I gambled on a late summer and lost. It rained every day for the whole of his first week and he had trenchfoot by Friday.

As Matthew is my younger, his arrival at school last year had implications for both of us. He had a new world to explore and conquer. All I have to do is remember to get only one plate out for lunch. I still forget. The thing you quickly discover when your children start school is not that the teacher will tell them everything they need to know but that they will tell the teacher everything you'd rather she did not know about life back at home. Every inner detail of your family's life will reach the teacher, either by word of mouth or by work of art.

On Matthew's first day at school he drew a picture of me. It looked like a smiling frying pan with two handles as seen from above, but it was in fact a representation of my salient features: a big smile in a round face on two legs. On day two he repeated this winning formula and painted an identical picture. On day three someone suggested he draw someone else for a change. So he drew Daddy . . . crying.

'Why is Daddy crying?' the teacher asked (and later reported to me).

'He banged his head on the wall,' he told her. This was a total fabrication, stated very confidently. The teacher was concerned. I could see the unspoken question in her eyes as she handed the picture over at the end of the day.

'Is Daddy psychotic or merely short-sighted?'

It is possible to get very paranoid about what the teacher thinks of you. In a sense it felt as if I was the one starting school. There are so many routines to learn: dinner slips, kit bags, reading books. It can all be rather daunting. You so much want to make a good impression, but the sole witness to all your sincere endeavours is a treacherous four-year-old who tells on you to teacher.

'Mummy said those dinner slips were a wetchid nuisance.'

'Mrs Brown, Mummy wrote all over that portent notice you said she had to read.'

'Mummy said, "Bother my reading book. We'll do it tomorrow."'

And so on and so on.

I suddenly found I had two sets of people to please: my children, who desperately wanted me to be normal (whatever that is), and their teachers, before whom I desperately feigned normality. It shouldn't have been so difficult. We are normal after all. But you don't feel normal when Mrs B. knows all about your family's way of life, as seen through the eyes of your child.

It can be very hard to stand your ground against such a tide of expectations. Last year I rebelled. One of the things I was expected to send in with my child on a daily basis, along with everything else, was a named purse containing a precise amount of pennies with which Matthew could purchase a drink at breaktime. If you have ever had to search for a particular combination of change regularly, you will know that all you can ever find around the house are those plastic pennies from toy cash tills. This might have added a whole new meaning to the question 'Do you take plastic?' but I retreated from the prospect of a stressful hunt every morning and made a policy decision that Matthew would manage through the morning without a drink. You may think me heartless, but I knew full well that by week two at least half of the other mummies would have given up sending in money.

At the end of the first day the teacher approached me. 'You forgot to send him with any money for a playtime drink.'

'No, I didn't forget. It was a policy decision,' I said, bravely swimming through the sea of guilt threatening to overwhelm me.

'Well, he was the only child with no pennies and

he did so want one . . .' She paused just long enough for me to drown in the aforementioned sea. '. . . So we gave him one.'

Great. Now Mummy is the old meanie and Mrs Brown is the ministering angel.

All this led to a great deal of confusion for poor Matthew, which left me regretting my rebellious stand against the teacher's instructions. Having once obtained a drink without pennies, he fiercely disputed with me that pennies were really necessary. As far as he was concerned, all you had to do to get a drink was to pull a sad face and look like you really needed one.

After a few days this ploy had obviously ceased to work because he told me that he had helped himself to one anyway.

'Matthew, that's stealing,' I pointed out.

'No, it isn't,' he explained patiently, 'because nobody saw me.'

Clearly we both have a lot to learn. For my part, I have to learn to trust Mrs B., my rival in his affections. For his part, he has to learn just how long the educational process will last. By the end of last September he'd reached the 'Is this optional?' phase.

'I think I'll stay at home next week, Mummy,' he announced. He was only four and three months, so who can blame him? He was missing his afternoon naps. He managed the occasional forty winks in the book corner but it wasn't the same. School started after breakfast when I left him there and finished when I reappeared, but in between the whole day was a blur of strange-sounding activities in strange-sounding places.

'In assembly today we took off our clothes and pretended we were walking through snow,' he told me one day. It sounded rather an odd assembly to me until I realised he'd got the act of worship confused with the act of exercise, as both took place in the big hall.

For years to come, September will represent one more step up the educational ladder. As Matthew's current ambition is to be a doctor in a 'hostipul' (where else?), 'in case you get ill, Mummy', I feel I should make every effort to support this gratifying concern for my future medical welfare. So I shouldn't resent all these September support services. I'd better turn out with my frying-pan smile and content myself with being the one fixed and reliable point in his constantly changing world.

Now, where did I put those name tapes?

Wednesday, 11 September

I'm really enjoying my study. After three years of working on the dining-room table with a cardboard box for a filing system, I just can't express the thrill it gives me to sit at a desk and pull open a drawer of my new filing cabinet, which came today. If we could afford it, I'd redecorate the room as well, but as we have neither the time nor the money, I have instead spent a happy morning covering as much of the vile flowery wallpaper as I can with all the framed photos I possess.

I love photographs. I now have all my favourite people on my study wall and lots of happy memories to distract me from work. Two pictures take pride of place. One is a family portrait of just the four of us taken three years ago for Mum's wedding. The second is a similar family portrait taken this year. The difference between these two pictures is that in the later one David and I look three years younger than we do in the earlier one and the children look three years older. We achieved this optical illusion by changing to contact lenses, in my case, and shaving off a moustache, in David's.

The only reason we had another portrait taken this year was because a skilled telesales person rang me at a vulnerable moment. I was so excited to be offered a discounted session, I took the bait. I did at least know the firm in question. On the day of the sitting the four of us went along with two outfits each and spent well over an hour being posed and positioned in a way that the photographer said would make us look like 'a united and relaxed family'.

The fact that we felt neither very relaxed nor very united didn't seem to bother him. We left the session thinking there was scant chance of success. Two weeks later I went back to see the results and a friend came with me. She had gamely volunteered to offer a second opinion and to restrain my spending to a reasonable limit. I knew we were in for the hard sell when we were ushered into a darkened room and our softly tinted photos were projected on to the wall while a soppy melody played in the background. Sensing that this was all designed to extract the maximum feeling of warmth from the prospective purchaser, I stiffened my resolve not to overspend.

My friend, meanwhile, dissolved. 'It must be my hormones,' she said, sobbing at a photo of the Bridge family.

Even my mother wouldn't do that.

The results were surprisingly good. Matthew, who had wriggled so much during the session, had also grinned wonderfully. Emma was her usual photogenic self, and even David and I didn't look as wooden as we'd felt.

In the end I compromised. Spending a little more than I'd anticipated, I purchased the medium-sized portrait that now hangs on my study wall. The price tag was hefty for a photo but a pittance for a memory.

Saturday, 14 September

This has not been a good week for transport. The car hasn't been running too well and David booked it into the garage for this morning. As he was about to depart on business for two weeks, it was up to the kids and me to get it there. I parked on the forecourt and left the kids to get out of the car by themselves while I went into the office to inform the mechanics of its arrival. As we had a mile and half's walk home, I was keen to get going.

'How will they move our car, Mummy?' Emma asked, a little way down the road.

'I've left the car keys in the ignition,' I explained, dangling the house keys in front of her face. There was a long pause while she weighed up her next question.

'How will they open the door to get in?'

I was about to explain that I'd left the doors unlocked but the words died on my lips as it dawned on me that my diligent and well-trained daughter had dutifully locked all the doors before leaving the vehicle. We had to go back and explain that leaving a locked vehicle with the keys inside was a simple oversight and not our idea of a good wheeze. I hope they don't charge me for the twenty minutes they spent finding a way in.

Sunday, 15 September – on technology

They sorted the car quite quickly yesterday once they'd got in. Even so, the figure at the bottom of the bill was the kind that makes me swallow hard and breathe quickly. At such moments all my anti-car instincts run riot and I seriously consider the option of selling it off and reverting to pedal power. Then I remember that my bike has a puncture and it's three miles to Sainsbury's.

Oblivious to my anti-car mood, Matthew has spent most of today making a car of his own. It is, in fact, a cereal packet covered in black paint and smothered with half a roll of Sellotape. It has a vertical exhaust pipe, made from half a loo-roll, and no wheels, so it could easily be mistaken for a steamship.

'The wheels were too much bother, Mum,' he explained. 'They kept falling off.'

I know just how he feels.

I do not qualify as that paradigm of modern parenthood, the techno-parent. A techno-parent can programme digital watches, the ones with two tiny buttons that reveal fifteen functions if you press them in a certain synchronised order. They carry pagers so their children can be in touch with them at all times. Techno-mummies weigh themselves (in kilos, of course) on high-tech scales; they work out in gleaming high-tech gyms; and they return to home-cooked dinners simmering in shiny, pre-programmed ovens.

I am not a techno-mummy. I have never mastered anything more technical than a tin opener. I can only tune the radio. My attempts to record *Playbus* used to result in half a foreign documentary. Technology has not only passed me by – it has run me over in the process. I have always had great difficulty in making inanimate objects co-operate with me –

objects like drinks machines or photocopiers. I have learnt that the secret is never to let them know you are in a hurry.

I stand in awe of anyone who can operate a photocopier. I don't mean someone who can merely press the green-for-go button. I mean people who can refill the paper cartridge or open the whole thing up to clear a paper jam. My first and last attempt to do the same for our simple printer at home resulted in my pulling out the entire printing mechanism along with the jammed paper, followed by six weeks of waiting for a replacement printer. And, yes, I did have the 'destructions' open at the correct page in front of me when I performed this feat.

When it comes to technology there are some of us with an aptitude and there are those of us with an attitude. I come into the second category.

My feeble attitude to anything technical makes me rather less than a paragon of Modern Motherhood. My excuse is that I am a pragmatist. I do not wish to know anything that I do not need to know. There isn't space in my mind for details like how to set the timer on my oven. I don't feel guilty or inadequate about this. I allow other people to bless me with their skills.

David has an aptitude for technology, which is very convenient. I firmly believe that women can be as technically competent as men, but in our family it so happens that all of the practical, mathematical and electronic skills are incarnate in my husband. He is our computer expert, our Mr Fix-it, and we do appreciate him. He can mend washing-machines, reprogramme computers and revive dead hair-driers. In my eyes this is akin to the gift of miracles.

This dependence on David is all very well until he goes away. In his absence I seem to struggle with all the technical gadgets that fill the home: the smoke alarms, the washing machine and the burglar alarm. The last item on that list is definitely the worst. I never really wanted a burglar alarm, but as David was prepared to do all the hard work of installing it, it seemed rather churlish to complain, so I left him to get on with it. The trouble is he is the only one who really understands how it works. The children were a little nervous of it at first, so we deliberately sited the control box at child height and taught them how to use it. The one drawback to this accessible system didn't reveal itself until a few weeks later, when a friend dropped by for a cup of tea. She had her little lad with her. Unfortunately, he is the sort of child who dismantles things for light entertainment.

He didn't discover the control box until he was about to leave, and even when he did give it a tentative tap, it warned him off with an irritated beep. As it appeared not to have reacted in any other way, I assumed all would be well when I came to set it at 3:08 on my way to fetch Emma from school at 3:10 (not so reckless as it sounds – the school is only two minutes away by bike).

However, I hadn't reckoned on the alarm system. Whichever button it was that had been pressed, it had set the system to automatic self-destruct mode. No sooner had I keyed in the first digit than the box outside burst into life with the full 95 decibels.

Half a minute's frantic reprogramming had no effect. The system had disowned me. Shouting at it irrationally, I realised I was fast running out of pedalling time. David had promised me that, should it ever go off unintentionally, he had set it to ring for only four minutes. So I hauled Matthew out from under the sofa cushions, where he had retreated (this was before he was at school), and reassured him, against all appearances to the contrary, that Mummy had everything under control. I plonked him on the back of the bike and pedalled madly away.

Any public-spirited person coming out to check whose alarm was ringing would have seen a harassed mother leaving the scene of the crime at top speed on a bicycle with a small child accomplice on the back. I may have been an unlikely-looking burglar, but I still felt very guilty, fleeing from the house with all the bells ringing! That was nothing compared to how guilty I felt when we sneaked home half an hour later only to find out that the alarm had blasted out for the maximum twenty minutes.

When we got into the house the control box was emitting a high-pitched scream. It was also ticking

'.... leaving the scene of the crime at top speed'

ominously. That did it. As both children headed under the sofa cushions, the gloves came off. My dismantling skills came into their own. Silence was regained and David was left to pick up the pieces. He didn't complain, much.

David's help has been invaluable in my ascent up the steep learning curve that faced me the day the home computer arrived. For the first few weeks I must have rung him twice a day at least. He tells me that computers are stupid and do only what you tell them to do, but I don't like to be reminded of this fact when I am fighting it out with a disobedient and unco-operative computer.

After the computer came the answerphone. I had resisted this piece of technology very hard, thinking of all the calls I'd have to return. I finally gave in and bought one for £3 at a car-boot sale because the man said it was easy to work. He was right. I can handle the incoming messages very nicely, thank you. It's leaving them for other people I find hard. My worst encounter with someone else's answer-machine was not long after we'd had our own installed. I was trying to call my editor at my publisher. I hadn't known him very long and was slightly in awe of him, so this was a fairly nerve-racking experience. I made it past the first post, the switchboard, and I was put through to his assistant. She told me that as he wasn't available at the moment, his 'voice mail' would take the call.

Think of me what you will. She may have said

'voice *mail*' but I heard 'voice *male*'. I was still thinking about this odd job description when a voice came down the line sounding for all the world just like the person I wished to speak to.

'Hello. Eric here,' it said. 'How can I help you?'

Several seconds into a stalled silence, it finally dawned on me what a voice mail was – just the answerphone – but was this it or had the voice mail been intercepted by the genuine article? He sounded awfully real to me, and his greeting was very direct.

Like an overloaded computer given too many variables, my brain crashed and out of the empty blankness came the only question which seemed to make any sense. 'Are you alive?'

'Yes,' he replied in the dignified, measured tone one normally reserves for small children or simpletons. He had paused barely long enough to check his pulse, as if this were the most natural opening question for any conversation. It took me several flustered sentences to regain my poise after that opening line.

No, I'm definitely not a techno-parent. I can only hope my everyday storytelling, face-wiping, tea-making, clothes-washing, bedroom-tidying skills make up for it.

Friday, 20 September

All this week Emma has been helping me across

roads. I have not suddenly reverted to infancy, nor have I lost my contact lenses. The reason for this role reversal is that she is very keen to walk to school on her own, but I'm not yet convinced that she has mastered the basics of road safety.

When you try to teach someone how to do a simple task, you suddenly realise how complicated it is. The 'Look right, look left, look right again' routine remembered from my childhood is hopelessly inadequate for our situation. Our route to school involves two main road junctions, so 'Look in five directions all at the same time' seems more appropriate, if somewhat impossible, advice. Our first task is to choose a good place to cross. This is complicated by the fact that parked cars are unavoidable at school drop-off time. Once we're in position I put her in charge of telling us when she thinks it's safe to cross. And then we wait . . . and wait . . .

She has had to learn to decode all the sometimes cryptic signals drivers give. An indicator light may (or may not) mean a car is going in a certain direction. But then again, a driver may still turn left, having failed to indicate. She has to judge by their speed and position in the road.

As if unreliable signalling wasn't enough to contend with, there is the problem of the drivers who slow down and wave her across the road in front them. I do wish they wouldn't do this. It's a big responsibility to call a child out on to a road. I know they mean well, and when we're in a hurry it's tempting to accept their offer, but it's hard for children to interpret an imperceptible wave of the hand and even harder to know whether to trust the adult driver. On the other hand, it seems very rude to tell kids to stand resolutely on the pavement and refuse to move. Matthew found the best solution for this problem this morning. He mistakenly assumed that the driver was just being friendly and he grinned and waved back.

Cars seem to have been the theme of this month. Ours has been playing up again and David is still away, which makes me nervous.

Monday, 22 September

The car didn't make it through the weekend. It gave up the ghost on Saturday evening. I'd only left the lights on for five minutes while I went into a shop and the battery gave up. Thankfully I live among Samaritans, all of them good. One friend came out and rescued me, took out the battery and put it on charge. When we discovered it was terminally flat, another friend loaned me a battery, but not before yet another friend had loaned me an entire car. In between all this sharing of resources two other friends gave me lifts. I felt truly cosseted.

With the car back in action (using the borrowed battery), I was able to drive the kids to school this morning when we were running late. I rarely drive them to school, so I parked, dropped them off, met a friend and walked home. It was only when I got home and looked at the empty drive that it occurred to me that I'd left the car at school.

I've had too many late nights. Without David's benign influence my night-owl tendencies have run riot. For the first few days it's fun to stay up beyond midnight and know I won't disturb him when I creep up into bed, but as forgetfulness sets in, the novelty wears off. I think I'll make a weary welcoming party for him when he returns on Saturday.

Friday, 27 September

Friday at last. David comes back tomorrow. I'm sure he's been working hard, but he's also been staying in the lap of luxury in classy hotels where the maid comes in to turn down the bed in the evening and leave some chocolates on the pillow. I hope he doesn't expect that when he gets home.

In his absence I have had exclusive rights to all the chores. My current chore is writing the shopping list, and I am struggling to think of dishes that will smooth his re-entry into ordinary life. I don't offer five-star cuisine. I'm hoping that toad-in-the-hole will seem sufficiently English, homely and welcoming.

It's felt like a long two weeks. When you are on your own some things become simpler: when Mummy says 'No' that's all there is to say on the matter. There's no other parental authority to appeal to. Most things become harder: I only have one person's quota of energy, one person's capacity to listen and I can only read one bed-time story at a time. The children have tolerated me pretty well, but I'm not so funny as their father and far less cheerful in the mornings. I'm also technically less competent and that has really been underlined this month. Still, at least I have kept them both safe. I haven't burnt too many dinners, nor have I lost my keys.

David was also away the day I had my worst experience to date with children, keys and cars. Matthew was only about eighteen months old at the time. I had parked the car outside our home to unload shopping and left Matthew snoozing in his car seat while I did so. After lifting out the final few bags and slamming the boot, I realised I had locked the car with Matthew and the keys inside.

Matthew opened his eyes with the first futile shake of the door handle. Strapped into his seat, unable to move and ready for his lunch, I realised it wouldn't be long before he would bawl his head off.

I raced round to the neighbours. The first one was out. The second one didn't have a phone. The third one, God bless him, rang for the police and gave me a toy car for Matthew to play with while he waited. It was only when I got back to the car that I realised that if I could have given the toy to Matthew I wouldn't have had a problem. Undaunted, I attempted to amuse him by driving it around the window nearest him.

The first police car that arrived brought two policeman. The second car brought a third. I felt that this was rather an excess of policemen attending to my small domestic crisis, but perhaps it was a quiet morning. I guess rescuing distressed mothers offers a lot of scope for noble endeavour. They took charge of the situation by asking if anyone had any equipment for breaking into cars. No one did. At least, they weren't going to admit it to the police. This flummoxed the officers for a bit, but they soon cheered up when someone offered to fetch a coat-hanger.

Quite a crowd had gathered. Matthew was getting fractious and I was feeling more than embarrassed. The policemen spent several minutes bending the coat-hanger and then asked everyone to avert their eyes while they broke in. No one did, which didn't matter because the coat-hanger trick didn't work. They obviously don't teach policemen how to be villains. Matthew was getting grumpier all the time, and I had to resort to singing his comfort song. Given his predicament, I had to sing at full volume. Not only did my loud and unaccompanied performance of 'Yes, Jesus Loves Me' do nothing for Matthew, it also did very little for my street cred. The situation was looking desperate. When the policemen came up with the idea of a truncheon through the window, I was ready to agree to anything. It was quick, painless and efficient but very pricy.

Locking a small child in a car by accident is something you do only once. I have since found several other means of rendering myself in need of the emergency services but, thankfully, not in these last two weeks. A bill for a new battery is the worst news that awaits David on his return. I think he'll cope.

Wednesday, 2 October

It's been one of those weeks already and it's only Wednesday. The list of things to get done each day has rivalled the length of my till receipt from Sainsbury's: people to ring, items to buy, letters to write, talks to prepare and people to see.

Out of all these tasks the first one feels the most difficult. Today I have no fewer than ten calls to make with messages as diverse as 'Yes, I'd love to come' (at the good end) and 'Why haven't you paid me?' (at the bad end). If I were to score my favourite activities on a scale of one to ten, making telephone calls would rate about minus five. If only this aversion had an effect on our phone bill.

This evening I am going to give a talk about being an imperfect parent in a town about an hour's drive away. I spent most of last night worrying about how to find the place and this morning a map came in the post. Penelope has agreed to come and keep me company, so as long as the car behaves itself we should be okay.

Thursday, 3 October

We got back at about half past eleven last night. The talk went well, I think. It amazes me that people are so keen to hear someone talking about all their own shortcomings as a parent. I guess it sends them away feeling better about themselves.

The car didn't let us down but the road system held us up. It normally takes ten minutes to get from our house to the motorway, but yesterday we had to navigate through roadworks and diversions and it took thirty minutes. Penelope had kindly offered to drive in view of the sleepless night I'd had the night before, but by the time she reached the motorway junction she was so disorientated she almost took the wrong slip road off the roundabout. Seeing us about to head north when we should have been heading south, I screamed very loudly. Fearing we were about to hit something or be hit, Penelope (who is a nervous driver at the best of times) slammed on the brakes and we stopped just in time. We spent the next twenty minutes shaking slightly and apologising to each other. After that the rest of the evening was a breeze.

Friday, 4 October

I didn't sleep very well again last night. There are too many things on my mental list of things to do and this causes my mind to go into overdrive. The whirring in my brain keeps me awake and when I finally get off the slightest noise wakes me up. This morning it was Emma's door creaking at five o'clock. Once I was awake my mind began to whirl again, going over the things on my list for today, all of which I could do much better if only I'd had a decent night's sleep. But I can't sleep because I've so much to do, and now I'm too tired to do anything because I've spent half the night worrying about all the things I have to do. And so on and so on.

One of the reasons for my disturbed sleep pattern is that the book I've written on how to keep your hair on when you've got too much to do (or *The Art of Plate Spinning*) comes out this month. I finished writing it a year ago, but it seems that I need to go back and take my own advice about sleep deprivation, exhaustion and hair loss (mine is falling out in handfuls).

Inefficiency sets in soon after sleeplessness and the evidence for this can be found in my diary for today. The only entry reads 'Twelve noon' and I haven't the faintest idea what is meant to be happening then. So much for running a well-organised life. Could it be a lunch guest? A dental appointment? A deadline? Should I stay in and be ready for anything or go out in the vain hope of finding myself in the right place at the right time? It has at least added an element of drama to the day but I expect to be disappointed.

A busy schedule isn't the only thing keeping me awake these nights: I am also experiencing a minor medical dilemma. I've been taking some painkillers for a pain in my neck and yesterday the doctor told me that the painkillers were the cause of the pain in my tummy. To cure the pain in my tummy I have to stop taking the stuff that cured the pain in my neck and start taking thrice-daily doses of something called Mucaine. (What a dreadful name. How on earth do they market the stuff? Why not just call it Vile and be done with it?)

In addition to giving up painkillers I have also had to wave goodbye to the chocolate, caffeine and custard doughnuts that have been my staple diet and say hello to rabbit food – muesli, celery and crispbread. My system is rebelling. The only consolation I have is that I may emerge from this regime slimmer and healthier – except, of course, for the pain in the neck and the bags under the eyes.

Saturday, 5 October – pets

Yesterday evening was awful. Emma got into a strop over something fairly minor, and after she'd whined on and on the whole thing blew up into a major row, which resulted in her being grounded for the evening. This meant she missed Girls' Brigade. We have never resorted to this particular sanction before and were astonished at its effectiveness. She got madder than ever and the whole miserable situation went on till almost ten o'clock. Episodes like this only serve to confirm my suitability as a spokesperson for the imperfect parent, but that thought offers little comfort at the time.

This morning I tried to refocus her mind on something more positive. She has been asking for a pet for several months now after I let her read an article about the pros and cons of pet ownership. I was trying to make her see that all pets have drawbacks, but she merely pointed out that the one she preferred had the fewest drawbacks.

What she really wanted was a kitten, but David has a proven allergy to cats, so she knew that she was on to a loser with that idea. A guinea-pig was out because we've done guinea-pigs (the overweight, geriatric Benjamin having finally given up the ghost in mid-feed back in February). Rabbits dig up the lawn, so David didn't want one of those, and I have an aversion to feathers and flapping, so that ruled out budgerigars. This left goldfish and stick insects still in the running, but both were rejected as not being sufficiently cuddly. Hamsters get full marks for cuddliness but lose out on personal hygiene (they smell). That left us with only one creature that seemed to meet all the criteria: a gerbil.

A few weeks ago we found a book in the library about gerbils. We discovered that they are clean creatures, eat very little, drink even less, reabsorb their own urine (how convenient) and as a result they hardly ever need cleaning out – the perfect pet! I could almost claim not to be influenced by the fact that they are also cheap and short-lived.

Feeling very pleased with ourselves that we had negotiated our way towards a mutually satisfying solution, Emma and I had set out to get the gerbil one weekend. This was the point where we began to discover the drawbacks. Gerbils, it seems, can be housed in wire cages which have a shallow tray at their base. The idea is that you fill the tray with sawdust and the gerbil, who loves to dig, spends its time merrily excavating the sawdust from the tray on to your floor. To avoid this problem you can house your gerbil in an old aquarium.

I was all for an aquarium. Emma wanted a cage.

My neighbour had both. She offered either to sell me the cage or to give me the aquarium, which was cracked. Emma still wanted the cage. Here we were, being offered hassle-free housing free of charge, and Emma *still* wanted the cage. She reasoned, she pleaded, she even promised to hoover her room every day, but she would not change her mind. We both dug our heels in and the stalemate has lasted for two weeks.

This morning I decided it was time to demonstrate some parental flexibility (in other words, I gave in).

She had accused me of not trusting her so, against my better judgment, I allowed her to go round to our neighbour's and buy the cage.

Next stop the pet shop.

Sunday, 6 October

David's mother and sister came for lunch today. It was quite a rush to get back from church in time to do a meal for everyone but good to see them all the same. We went out to a garden centre in the afternoon and Emma was delighted to find there was a pet shop next door.

Having got the cage yesterday, she was keen to work her way down her shopping list: sawdust, food, water bottle and gerbil. If this were show business I'd stand full square behind the adage 'Never work with children and animals', but it isn't. This is family life, and the combination of the two seems obligatory at some stage. We had, at least, agreed on just the one gerbil. It is notoriously difficult to tell the boys from the girls and getting a mixed pair by mistake is a nightmare. The females are fertile every five days, give birth four weeks later and those babies can breed again within weeks. Knowing how to separate the lads from the lasses is essential if you don't want an exploding gerbil population in your living room.

The shop had all the right gerbil accessories and

a clutch of cute-looking gerbils. Emma was very excited about finally getting to choose one. Unfortunately, we forgot to ask the sex of our gerbil, so when we got home we got the book out and had a go at finding out for ourselves, but as the difference is only about two millimetres, we're not entirely sure. Emma has opted for the feminine gender but is sticking with a neutral name just in case.

Wednesday, 9 October – of grandmothers

We've had a recent rush of grandmothers. David's mum was here on Sunday and my mum dropped in for the day today. The children distinguish between my mother and David's mother by giving them different titles and defining epithets: my mother is 'Grandma who comes with Grandpa Bill' and David's mother is 'Gran who comes on the train'. The children are equally delighted to see either of them.

This time, though, my mother was on her own. Grandpa Bill was at home convalescing. She came in her car as usual. This allows her to transport as large a proportion of her wardrobe as the boot will allow. She has a weakness for bags and shoes. A whole case will be devoted to shoes, but she will wear only one pair throughout her visit and buy at least one more pair if you happen to pass a shoe shop. Then on the last day she will leave her original shoes under the settee and set off home in a totally different pair. I wouldn't mind but I don't fit a size 3.

We had a good time together today. For once we took ourselves to a proper shop and bought some furniture for the extension. Second-hand shops are our more usual haunt, as my mother is a whizz at recycling. She once went to a wedding wearing an Oxfam hat inside out because she liked the colour of the lining. Nobody noticed . . . until I told them!

Hospitality was easy because the house was well stocked with cakes, biscuits and chocolates. This was because 'Gran who comes on the train' had been here on Sunday. 'Gran who comes with a cake' would be as good an epithet for David's mum. She adores all things sweet and sticky in the culinary line. Before we went to France I overheard her telling the children the most important French words to remember were 'gâteau' and 'éclair'.

She is also good with vegetables, although these aren't so popular with the kids. Visits to Gran's have a ritual all of their own: electric blankets warm the beds for at least twelve hours before our arrival, fresh vegetables boil on the stove and a coffee cake with walnuts waits for us in the larder.

This routine is set to change as Gran is about to move house, a major upheaval for her as she has lived in the same house for thirty years. She

'Gran who comes on the train'

has saved many of David's old toys; my kids now play with the old box of Lego, and even his elderly Action Man has returned to active duty. This week she brought more things she has unearthed in her clear-out as well as a pile of paperwork for David to read through.

It's a wise decision to settle yourself into a smaller house before the large one becomes a problem, but it's also quite a wrench leaving a home you have lived in for most of your life, the home where your children grew up. She's only moving two hundred yards down the street, so that helps, and I'm sure once the dust settles none of the important things will have changed: there'll still be electric blankets in the beds, vegetables on the stove and a cake in the cupboard.

Friday, 11 October

Emma has been taking pet-ownership very seriously. Sandy seems to have settled in, and Emma has been very attentive to her every need. She is not quite so attentive to the sawdust on the floor. She has hoovered her room several times, I must admit, but not before the trail of sawdust has stretched to the landing and halfway down the stairs.

She is still reading up on gerbils, and this evening she shared with me a list of variations we could make to Sandy's diet. 'Gerbils can eat fresh fruit and vegetables, bananas and apples,' she read, 'but remember that all wild vegetarians should be washed and dried thoroughly before use.'

The word was 'vegetation' but I was highly amused and toyed with the idea of posting up a warning on her bedroom door: 'Wild vegetarians will be thrown to the gerbil.'

Poor Matthew has been quietly observing this pet-owning process. Now that all his sister's pet longings are fulfilled, his own are harder to bear. Lately he has taken to making jam-jar wormeries and keeping slugs in drawers, but his real yearning in life is to have a dog.

The problem is that the head of our household has an unproven allergy to dogs. I say 'unproven' because he merely thinks he might be allergic. As we have had several dogs to stay recently and David hasn't yet broken out in spots or wheezes, we're getting suspicious.

This week Matthew told David that, yes, he did love him very much but he would love him even a bit more if he wasn't related to dogs (he meant 'allergic' but he couldn't say it). I could see David's resistance to the dog idea giving way in the face of such blatant pressure.

Matthew covets every dog in the neighbourhood. We have to stop and say hello to every pooch we encounter all the way to school and back. I am now getting to know the local dog-owners fairly well. I could be easily persuaded to have a dog of our own but David has never had a dog and may take some winning over.

Sunday, 13 October

It was our Harvest Family Service at church this morning, so I dug up a dead tree from the garden and took it to church with us. I'd been saving the dead tree especially for today. It wasn't part of our harvest contribution; it was a visual aid for my sermon. I hadn't killed the tree deliberately. It had conveniently died of natural causes, the most obvious of which was the fact that it was planted in our garden.

I'd really sweated over this morning's talk. Sermons at all-age services can be an uphill effort. You have to say something that will be as relevant to a five-year-old as to a fifty-year-old. As if this weren't hard enough, you also have to use words of no more than three syllables, be visual and interactive and never take longer than ten minutes. If you're using a good Bible story, it helps.

This morning we didn't have a story, we had a concept: fruitfulness. The Family Planning Group took on this theme as a challenge. For the first five-minute talk slot they developed a quiz in which several volunteers had to match seeds to the correct produce. This was amazingly successful considering the fact that all the volunteers were under ten.

For the second talk slot they suggested the dead-tree idea. At the time this seemed to be an original, creative, if slightly wacky notion. This morning, when we were struggling to get a six-foot conifer into a five-foot car and then attempting to repot it in the church vestibule, it felt like a very silly idea indeed.

It was meant to be a visual aid for the reading 'I am the Vine; you are the branches. If a man remains in me and I in him, he will bear much fruit' (John 15:5). The connection between a fruitful vine and a dead Christmas tree isn't immediately obvious: one was meant to be the opposite of the other. The point is that, unlike a vine, a Christmas tree has no roots. It is merely a sawn-off stump, so it has no way of drawing life from the soil. It ends up dry, barren and lifeless and no amount of dressing it up with baubles and lights can revive it. I took along some baubles to prove my point.

Matthew had been very excited to see the Christmas decorations coming down from the loft. Adorning my dead tree in mid-sermon was my bid to be visual. The congregation tolerated this time-warp out of respect for a good illustration, but I'm sure all the five-year-olds went home to write their letters to Father Christmas.

At least it was different. Hardly a radical alternative to the wholemeal images commonly found in traditional harvest services, but we tried. Next time I think we'll stick to a story.

Friday, 18 October

After two weeks on the vile medicine three times a day, my stomach is finally improving. My neck isn't too bad and I'm sleeping a little better. My hair is still falling out, but you can't have everything. Yesterday I felt well enough to throw an impromptu dinner party for eight. I hadn't meant to but when the church event to which we had invited our friends was cancelled at short notice, I asked them all back here for a meal. This on a day when I had nothing in the freezer and no means of transport to Sainsbury's.

What the heck. No one seemed to mind the concoction of thrown-together store-cupboard standbys. The company mattered much more than the food. We had such a good evening I wish I had the courage to do it more often.

Sunday, 20 October – of kids in cars

We have stopped at Gran's *en route* to our half-term break in north Yorkshire.

This morning was very stressful. Not only did we have to have everything we needed for our three days away loaded into the car before church (so that we could make a quick getaway afterwards) but we also had to be there early because I was in charge of Sunday school. It was my job to open up the venue.

We arrived at church late with the car loaded and at least one of the children boiling over with fury about some last-minute hassle. I didn't think things could get any worse, but then I opened up the Sunday-school venue and discovered a break-in. The Sunday-school rooms weren't affected, so my only problem was how to get thirty children and a similar number of parents in and out of the place around all the officials, police and scene-of-crime officers who turned up within minutes. This had to be the morning I had arranged for a special visitor to come to Sunday school. She was a local midwife and she had come to talk to the children about her job and her faith. She had brought a pregnant mum with her and used her hand-held heartbeat monitor to let us all hear the baby. Then she showed us a blood-pressure kit and tried it out on me. Given the morning I'd had, my reading should have been off the scale, but it was reassuringly low. Maybe my stress levels are not so bad after all.

We arrived here in time for lunch and have spent the afternoon with Gran. She is feeling rather despondent about her house sale. She still can't decide whether she really likes the house she is buying, and the finality of it all has really got to her. I'm sure she's had a few sleepless nights over it and I wish there was some way to make it easier for her.

We are driving north in the morning to meet up with some friends and spend a few days walking together. We have hired an outdoor centre and are going to self-cater. I use the word 'we' loosely. I haven't actually planned, booked or cooked anything – the very idea gives me a headache. We are simply blessed with friends who can do that sort of thing standing on their heads. They have kindly invited us and about twenty-five others to tag along.

I hope the children will cope with the long car journey in the morning. Every parent has their own personal horror story about children on long journeys. 'Sick every ten minutes in a three-hour jam on the M5' is the kind of situation we all dread. Emma was complaining of a poorly tummy before bedtime tonight.

Our worst experience in a car was the aforementioned drive to the South of France when the children were tiny. My mind has mercifully blanked out most of this traumatic experience, but David recalls that at several points in the journey he was the only occupant of the vehicle not in tears. Our return journey was only a little better. As if to prove that the longest journey begins with the smallest step, we had gone a mere three miles when a little voice from the back piped up, 'Is this the road to Grandma's house?'

'Sort of, we replied. 'Just another 950 miles to go.' Whoever said that to travel hopefully is better than to arrive had never travelled with small children, for whom the moment of arrival is undoubtedly the best part of any journey.

Tomorrow's journey is a mere two hours up the A1, so we shouldn't have too many problems. I remember thinking when the children were smaller how useful some kind of signalling system would be: lights maybe, or a message board in the rear window that would allow me to inform fellow drivers of my predicament. The words 'Tantrum in progress' or 'Toilet needed *now*' would go a long way to explaining my frenzied break from the outside lane to the hard shoulder or my sudden loss of clutch control.

From the children's point of view on the back seat, I guess we adults must seem like dictators. We strap them in and drive them round without giving them the opportunity to choose when and where they'd like to stop, eat or relieve themselves. When Emma was four I recall driving her past a school, pointing it out to her and reminding her that she would soon be going to school. All the frustrated powerlessness of being on the back seat came out in her reply: 'Yes, and then there will be three of us who can drive in this family.'

I had to break it to her gently that driving did not yet form part of the National Curriculum, at least not for the rising fives. Disappointed, her vision of sitting in the driving seat, with all its connotations of power, rapidly fading, she has since had to content herself with back-seat driving. Mind you, I can hardly blame her for being vigilant. Driving with Mummy can be a stressful experience. Not for nothing have we developed the habit of in-car prayers before any long journey. At such times both of my children will pray very specifically with great enthusiasm.

'Don't let Mummy get lost.' (This after a directional error on the M6. How should I know which way is south? I'm a mother, not a homing pigeon.)

'May we not run out of petrol.' (This after an episode involving steep embankments, high fences and muddy fields.)

'May we not break down.' (So far, so good on this one.)

'May we not drive off the road.' (Ditto.)

'. . . fall out of windows.'

'. . . drive off cliffs.'

Their imaginations get the better of them after a while.

Having prayed for delivery from all these potential disasters they are actually quite calm on most journeys. This may be due to child-like faith or it could be just that they are a bit older now.

For tomorrow's journey we are well stocked with tapes, books and snacks to consume on the way. The only thing likely to disturb their peace is David's optimistic habit of pointing out any and every obscure object of interest that we happen to pass. Most drivers with experience of chauffeuring small children will know that this is a dangerous pastime, worth engaging in only if your children are very bored or the object is very large and interesting.

One has to calculate carefully the likelihood of one's small passengers actually being able to see the object, having learnt from experience that 'Look, there's a tractor' is usually followed by 'No, over *there.* Look the other way. No, not that way, this way!' Failure to see the cow/tractor/pig/man with funny hat can lead to a bad case of the miseries on the back seat.

On one occasion my husband pointed out a hugely obvious object of dubious interest (a water tower) which approached us at 50 miles an hour and disappeared at the same rate. Having craned his head round the full 360 degrees to no avail, my despondent young son asked the impossible question: 'Did *I* see it?' The poor little fellow wouldn't have known what a water tower looked like even if he'd sat on one.

He does, however, know what planes look like, but they are even harder to spot, especially as my keen plane-spotter husband encourages the use of a rather military method of describing their location. For those of you unfamiliar with this method 'twelve o'clock' is the spot on your bonnet where Blithe Spirit would sit if you drove a Rolls (which we don't). Thus one parent will shout out, 'Nine o'clock,' or 'Eleven o'clock,' which will immediately cause the other parent to crane his or her head round at a dangerous right angle to the road.

It just goes to show that children are not the only ones who behave strangely in cars.

Monday, 21 October

The journey was almost without incident: with half an hour to go, Emma threw up in the back of the car. We cleaned her up on the hard shoulder and got here at about two o'clock. She seemed okay, so we set off with the crowd to explore some local rocks.

There were rather a lot of them and they just begged to be climbed. The chaps and the children did most of the climbing until I decided to attempt an ascent of my own. It didn't look very difficult . . . from the ground. Twenty feet up and wedged in a crevice, I thought it was very difficult indeed. Those below me tried the laying on of hands to no effect (i.e., they shoved me), so it was left to several men above to haul me up by my arms. This seemed to be a very entertaining spectacle for those on *terra firma*. Thankfully only my dignity was dented and I made it safely down.

Tuesday, 22 October

Today's activity was a seriously long walk. Seriously long for suburban types like us, that is. Normally the suggestion 'Let's go for walk' brings our children out in a rash of complaints: 'Do we have to?' 'How far are we going?' 'Are we nearly there?'

Today, given ten other children for company, they managed six and half miles without a single moan. They were all still skipping along at the end of the day when the proximity of a teashop was the only thing keeping most of us adults going.

There were no difficult rocks this time – only one slippery one that brought one of our party painfully to the ground about half a mile from home. The bad news was that she couldn't move. The very bad news was that we were in a field of bulls. The good news was that we had a casualty sister with us who was carrying a full first-aid kit. The ankle was strapped and painkillers administered quicker than you could say 999. Michael Buerk would have been impressed.

Wednesday, 23 October

This morning Plan A had been to visit a show cave, but then the sun came out and we switched to Plan B: exploring a local gorge. The gorge had a stream and some more slippery rocks. We walked along the rocks and one of our group fell into the stream, much to everyone's amusement. Then we explored a cave, which was rather more primitive than the show cave we'd intended to visit. It had no lights or paths, just water running down the walls and an exit at both ends. It was about fifty feet long, pitch-dark and very narrow in places. We had two torches, five eager children and five less eager adults. The worst bit was where you had to turn sideways to wriggle between the rocks. Fresh air and daylight have never looked so good. I declined the return trip through the other way.

I sat on the grassy bank above the cave and thought about the Psalms. 'He leads me beside quiet waters' . . . but doesn't push me in, and 'He set my feet on a rock' . . . but thankfully not a slippery one. It's been a very restorative few days.

Sunday, 27 October

The holiday effect hasn't lasted. Today I am as stressed as I have been all month. I bungled Sunday school this morning and feel fed up and tearful about the demands life is making of me at the moment. One good thing that happened today was a trip to the local RSPCA kennels to look for a suitable dog. David is coming round to the idea and I keep telling him that pet-ownership is very good for stress levels.

Tuesday, 29 October

I went to the doctor's today to talk about my hair falling out. She sent me for some blood tests but said it's probably all to do with my stomach complaint. Little does she or anyone else know the pressures I've battled with this month. Still, I'll go for the tests anyway and we'll see.

Wednesday, 30 October

I rang a close friend today only to find out that her husband was hit by a lorry yesterday. Most of the bones down his left side are broken and he's not out of danger yet. The prospect of losing a dear friend who would leave three young children and wife bereaved brought me rapidly out of my slough of self-pity and on to my knees.

Yesterday I heard that our friend who fell over on the walk in Yorkshire last week hadn't merely sprained her ankle. The doctor confirmed today that she'd broken it, and she's now in plaster for the next six weeks. And to think I was worrying about hair loss. Pathetic, isn't it?

Thursday, 31 October

Ruth and John are here on a flying visit. They came this evening and are only staying one night. The last time I saw Ruth was back in July, when David came home with the news that he'd been offered a job in Lancashire. In the intervening time we have built the extension, taken on new roles at church and all but forgotten about the possibility of moving away. Well, I at least had done my utmost to forget about it.

David came in from work this evening not long after Ruth and John had arrived and told us that the firm in Lancashire had got in touch again today to firm up the details of the job offer. Suddenly a move north is back on the agenda; the details are all much more concrete than we'd expected. It's also a promotion and they want him to start early next year. I just can't get over the timing of this news and the fact that once again Ruth is here. It was good to talk through our initial reactions and fears.

Friday, 1 November

This morning, after Ruth and John had left, I went dog hunting. Earlier in the week I'd discovered a breeder who told me that his dogs have a bomb-proof temperament. This sounded ideal for family life and, combined with the fact that this type of dog is small, doesn't shed hair and needs only a little exercise, I felt it was certainly worth doing some research. This morning's trip had a touch of escapism about it, but it felt luxurious to set off on my own in the car and have some peace and quiet to think.

I don't know what to make of this new job that David has been offered. Is it a new direction or a distraction from everything that's been going on here? If we go, it'll be the tenth time I've moved in the thirty-four years of my life. Part of me is so used to moving on, I can't help feeling a thrill of excitement at the thought of a new place to discover, but another part of me feels that it would cut short all that we've got going for us here and might unsettle the children. Moving four or five times in my own childhood has made me a very independent, 'talk to anyone' sort of person and broadened my view of the world, but at the same time it has affected the way I form relationships and I recognise that I make good friends very slowly as a result. The upsetting thing is that I've made quite a few good friends over the five years we've lived here and I don't really want to start all over again.

The hour's drive to the breeder allowed me to think through these conflicting emotions and then I shoved them to one side. The puppy was gorgeous; I fell for him at once. He looked more like a tousled antique teddy bear than a dog. The breeder listened sympathetically to my concerns about David's unproven allergy and even offered to take the puppy back if things didn't work out. That clinched it. I arranged to collect the dog a week on Saturday. All the way home I thought about names for him. He's currently called Ben, but as we know several Bens of the human variety, we'd like to rename him. I hope this won't give him an identity crisis.

The children were wildly excited when we told them at teatime and several alternative names were suggested, not all of them sensible. Chester seemed to be the favourite. Quantum, as in quantum leaps, is the least likely. David assured us that 'quantum' means 'a small bundle of energy' and he's a physicist so he should know, but I ruled it out on the basis that the dog's legs are too short for leaping and I'd feel very silly yelling, 'Quantum!' from the back door.

Sunday, 3 November

I couldn't sleep last night. Partly I was excited about the dog and partly I was fretting about moving to Lancashire. By this morning I was so weary and befuddled that I forgot to put the dinner in the oven before we left for church. This wouldn't have mattered very much were it not for the fact that a family of four were expecting to have lunch with us, preferably cooked. I remembered just before the last hymn and made a speedy exit. We ate late and no one was any the wiser. I think I got away with it.

Monday, 4 November

Whoever it was who said, 'A change is as good as a rest,' wasn't a parent, particularly not a parent organising a few days away from home on her own. Tomorrow I am to go down to Brighton with a group from church to attend a conference until Friday.

The logistics of leaving the family to fend for itself are complicated at the best of times, but David has just announced that he will also be away on business for two of the three nights that I am away. This will leave the children here on their own with a parent at either end of the country. This morning I contemplated cancelling but instead I called in the cavalry. Gran has kindly agreed to come down and hold the fort for us, take the children back and forth to school, make the tea and even do the ironing. God bless her.

She has had this role in the past on several occasions, but this will be her first time doing an overnight shift with all its consequent morning joys of jollying children into school uniform and packing lunch boxes. I sat down to write her a few notes this afternoon. Four sides of A4 later, I thought I'd covered everything. The mine of information required to run a standard week of family life amazed me: 'Violin on Thursday', 'Swimming kit on Friday', 'Beavers on Wednesday'. The clauses and subclauses, complete with phone numbers, went on and on.

I feel I have prepared for every eventuality on the home front. I've even highlighted all the appropriate children's programmes in the TV guide. I haven't left myself any time to pack my own clothes, but I'm sure it won't take long in the morning.

Tuesday, 5 November

I forgot everything. I forgot my packed lunch, the map, my sunglasses. I even forgot to turn off the

M1 when I reached the M25. In spite of these setbacks I still reached Brighton three and half hours after I set out. I called home this evening and all is well apart from the fact that the telly blew up after school. So much for highlighting the programme guide.

Friday, 8 November – of new babies and new beginnings

I got home just before the children came out of school today. I stopped to buy a dog basket on the way because tomorrow we fetch the dog. The TV had indeed exploded in a terminal but not dangerous fashion. Everything else had run smoothly: the children had excelled themselves; Gran had done a sterling job; and the ironing lay neatly folded over the chairs.

I'm so glad I didn't cancel at the last moment. I had a brilliant time away. It did me so much good to be with a group of stompingly joyful Christians, singing their heads off and soaking in the Spirit. They might have been too stompingly joyful for some people's tastes, but after the stresses of last month, I felt like a brick being dropped into a bucket of water and letting the water slowly soften it. (I know bricks don't go soft in water but this a metaphor not a factual description.) The teaching was good and the atmosphere of faith and expectancy really lifted me.

I went forward for prayer at the end of one session, really just to dump at God's feet all the heavy loads I'd been carrying these last few weeks. The woman who prayed for me said she felt there was light at the end of the tunnel. Whenever someone says that David always quips that it's probably a train coming the other way. I thought about him and about the Lancashire job and wondered what to make of it all. As an unexpected bonus my stomach problem has cleared up completely and I didn't even pray about that.

This week David's sister, Becky, announced that she's expecting her first child. Gran has got the knitting needles out already. We rang to congratulate Becky and Paul this evening. Being pregnant for the first time is one of those experiences that plunges you into a cauldron of joy, fear, confusion, delight, apprehension and anxiety. Talking to Becky tonight brought it all back. It seems as if we were at the same stage only yesterday. She was talking about going for her first antenatal appointment. I have never forgotten mine. What an initiation it was!

I had arrived early, and though I was only twelve weeks pregnant I was already wearing a tent (you can't wait the first time). I felt like a ship in full sail on a voyage of discovery into the unknown. Little did I know that the main concern of the nursing staff would be my maiden name, not my maiden voyage.

At first they couldn't find any record of my

appointment. This was because I had coyly over-looked telling the receptionist that I was pregnant. She couldn't find me in the 'Male Patient' book, nor the 'Female Patient' book. The problem was resolved when I owned up to my condition and was found in the 'Pregnant Female' book.

I'd just settled down to wait when I was called into another area, where I handed over the full jam jar which had been discreetly tucked into my handbag. (Full? Well, how was I to know how much they'd need?)

Having dealt with the sample, the nurse worked her way through a bewildering list of checks and questions while simultaneously moving around the room and in and out of the cubicles at great speed. Maybe she is doing three of us at once, I thought. At any rate, I was the only one responding to her questions.

Weight?

Height? (Help! Do I get smaller or taller in pregnancy?)

Urine. (The jam jar. We'd done that bit.)

Blood pressure.

Maiden name?

Phone number?

Occupation?

Sign here.

Maiden name?

Blood group?

Rubella test?

And, finally, maiden name?

Perhaps the maiden-name question was some kind of test to see if I was disorientated by the way she was moving around the room. Or maybe she just forgot to write it down in the first place.

'That's all from me then,' she finally announced. 'The midwife and doctor will see you now.'

'You mean there's more?' I felt like I'd already gone three rounds in the ring.

The midwife turned out to be a large, red-faced lady, very out of breath, who cheerfully steam-rollered me through a physical examination. She advised me about diet, varicose veins and heartburn while demonstrating (on me, I might add) how to roll one's nipples in preparation for breast feeding.

By the time the doctor reached me there really wasn't much left that hadn't already been copiously noted down. However, I did get to ask a few questions of my own. As the doctor completed the final few forms and I prepared to leave, the wheezy midwife leaned over the table and asked me one last time, 'What was your maiden name again?'

Yes, I remember it well and am heartily glad not to be going through it all again. It's not just the indignity of labour; it's the uncertainty of early parenthood that's so nerve-racking. We spent the first evening that Emma was at home hovering over the pram debating whether or not she was too hot in a vest, a nightie *and* a cardigan. 'Should we remove the cardigan?' became a life-or-death decision, which we finally resolved by ringing my older and wiser sister some thirty miles away. How on earth I expected her to assess the temperature of our lounge from that distance, goodness only knows. She kindly gave us some guidelines and didn't laugh (at least not until she'd put the phone down), which was a good thing because such a small anxiety seemed utterly overwhelming at the time.

I'm glad I'm no longer a new mum, but the experience I've gained so far doesn't help much with all the new decisions and dilemmas that face us now. Motherhood is one long maiden voyage. I'm still finding myself in new situations where I'm not sure what to do. I shall still be waiting for the parcel labelled 'experience' the day the children walk out the door as fully fledged adults.

Sunday, 10 November

We fetched the dog yesterday morning. The children were utterly delighted. The dog wasn't quite so sure about the arrangement. One hour in the back of the car with the kids and he'd thrown up twice and relieved himself in every possible manner. This he has continued to do anywhere and everywhere ever since we got home. The stair gate has gone up to teach him not to go upstairs and the newspaper has gone down to teach him that there are some places you may puddle and some places you may not.

We're calling him Ben *and* Chester at the moment and hope to drop the Ben in a day or two. He whimpered dreadfully last night when we left him and refused to sleep in his bed. When I came down this morning he was in the comfy chair, on which he promptly puddled as I approached. He was sick again after breakfast and I felt a bit panicky. I had to ring my sister and ask her what to do with a sick dog. They got a new dog last year so she knows all about it.

This is early motherhood all over again! Toilet training, stair gates, teething, broken nights, mopping up puke . . . It's just as well he's adorable. We had several visitors today and he coped fairly well until disaster struck two hours ago. Emma leaned over the stair gate to pat him goodnight and the gate gave way. She and the gate fell on top of the dog, who yelped loudly and has limped ever since. Poor Emma was very upset and she wasn't the only one. The dog doesn't seem to be in any pain, but if the limp hasn't gone by tomorrow I guess we'll have to head for the vet. We've only had him two days!

Monday, 11 November

The vet gave Chester the okay. He also told us to put his collar on and leave it. He's never had a collar on before and whenever I've put it on he behaves pitifully, as if I've punished him.

Thursday, 14 November

It has been three whole days and he has finally stopped sulking about his collar. Attaching a lead to it is the next hurdle. The children are desperate for him to walk to school with them, but whenever I clip on the lead he just stands rooted to the spot and shakes. I need to discover the doggy version of 'giddy up'. Today I phoned a helpful dog-training lady and she advised me just to take it slowly.

Monday, 18 November

What a difference a day makes. Yesterday was the murkiest, wettest November day so far and we were stuck indoors with two children and an antisocial dog (the dog wasn't really antisocial – we just haven't cracked house-training yet). He won't even go out in the garden on his own.

This meant that yesterday I had to spend several long spells outside in my wellies and warm coat, complete with umbrella, escorting the dog around all the trees and bushes in our garden, hoping he'd find one of them acceptable.

He didn't. He preferred the green carpet in the hall. He's also still refusing to walk with a lead.

Today, however, the sun is shining, the skies are a glorious blue and I feel 100 per cent more positive about this training business. I'm going to take the puppy down to the towpath later and we *will* go for a walk. Blow this 'take it slowly' lark.

Yesterday's weather seemed to reflect my recent experience. Things have been dark and gloomy around here for some time. The future looks uncertain; the diaries have been too full; minor illnesses have got us down; and the normal stresses of home, church and work responsibilities have felt too heavy. The crises of several close friends have caused us concern. Thankfully my friend who was hit by the lorry is now out of danger, but recovery will be very slow. In spite of this good news, I have to be honest and admit that life at the moment feels fairly faith-draining.

The sunshine this morning lifted me a bit and reminded me of heaven. If I'm going to keep the day-to-day realities of life in perspective, I must keep my hopes, expectations and motivation firmly connected to eternal realities. Whatever else happens, in no more than seventy years from now I'll be in heaven. When you put it like that it doesn't seem so bad.

In my readings I am continually being reminded that life is a journey and that we have to move on. This isn't exactly what I want to hear just at the moment, what with this decision about Lancashire hovering over us, but it does help me to think about heaven when the 'yuck' of life really gets to me. Heaven reminds me that God can intervene; he can transcend the mess of life and transform it. The difference between yesterday's gloom and today's sunshine reminds me of that.

Yesterday I asked the children what they thought heaven would be like. Emma thought about it carefully and then, with brilliant insight, summed up Revelation 21 in six words: 'No first-aid kits in heaven.'

From the mouths of babes . . .

Tuesday, 19 November

The dog now walks. The towpath did the trick. I took him to a particularly soft and squelchy part, attached the lead, turned my back and pulled. By the time he'd done five yards on his nose through the mud, he'd discovered what his legs were for. Now there's no stopping him. The kids are so pleased – he walked to school with us today.

We are no nearer a decision about the Lancashire job. I can tell David is fairly keyed up about it, but there doesn't seem much point in discussing it, as we won't know any more until next Monday when someone from up there is coming down to meet him. I was reading last night about some Old Testament characters, all of whom made plans in good faith but none of them worked out. 'For

'The dog now walks'

my thoughts are not your thoughts, neither are your ways my ways,' said Isaiah (55:8). I wish it was easier to get on to God's wave length. Whenever I peer into the future in prayer, clutching all my plans, hopes and dreams in my sweaty palms, God's only reassurance is that he knows the plans he has for me (Jeremiah 29:11); in other words, the future is in his hands, not mine. If I want to receive his plans, then I know I need to put down my own hopes and expectations and lift up empty, undemanding palms of expectant trust.

You'll have to help me loosen my grip, Lord.

Wednesday, 20 November

I had to go for the test on my stomach today, the one the doctor sent me for in October. I tried very hard to get out of it by ringing and explaining that I've been fine for weeks now, but the doctor insisted. The test involved a long, thick black tube, a degree of sedation, a loss of dignity and a day in hospital, but I'll spare you the details. By passing on the sedation I was able to cut down the stay in hospital to two hours. Although the procedure was more than a little uncomfortable, being awake for five minutes of misery outweighed the nuisance of leaving the dog on his own for the whole day. It's also true that I've never been sedated in my life and I really didn't fancy the idea. I like to know where I am and what's happening to me at all times. I guess I'm just a control freak.

Saturday, 23 November

Small boys under the age of eight ought to come fitted with a volume-control knob. We have had two on the premises this weekend, one of our own and the son of our friend in hospital. Whatever the boys are doing, they do it at full volume: talking, fighting, singing, playing, fighting some more and even eating. Everything comes with added decibels. At least I am not left wondering where they are.

I've found it very entertaining to eavesdrop on their conversation – not that eavesdropping was really necessary. It has consisted almost entirely of the exchange of one-liners plucked straight from the pages of *Beano*:

'Howzat!' (Lunging for lower legs.)

'That'll stop ya!' (Hiding toy from rival.)

'Gotcha on the brain box!' (Administering blow to head.)

'Arrgh!' 'Vroom, broom! 'Erk! 'Yeeha!' 'Yikes!' and 'Splat!' (Expressions of pain, delight, victory or frustration depending on the circumstances.)

The boys seem to have no trouble understanding one another in spite of this return to fairly primitive communication. They've had a whale of a time.

Emma, by way of contrast, has excelled herself with girliness all weekend. By this afternoon she'd had enough of the sword-wielding brigands and their pirate ship (Matthew's bed) and shut herself in the kitchen to cook.

In my absence she turned out some very edible oat cookies and some fluorescent pink fairy-cakes (slight accident with the cochineal). The fruits of her industriousness were gleefully consumed by the pirates when they'd had their fill of plundering the bedroom.

She enjoyed the baking, the boys enjoyed the eating, so everyone was happy – well, almost everyone. I was left with the washing-up. Thus all the traditional gender roles were soundly reinforced: boys make a mess and have huge appetites; girls make a mess but more creatively; and mummies clear away everyone else's mess.

Mess would be a fair description of the house at the moment and not just because of occupants of the small male variety. Our motivation for decorating has nosedived since moving became a possibility, so we are still living with the bare plaster walls and concrete floors of the extension. Not that it really matters. A concrete floor is an asset when it comes to house-training a puppy (huge improvement in that department).

I think that mess is a good metaphor for life: relationships are complex, people are awkward, accidents happen, decisions are unclear and no one is perfect. If I want to live peacefully and love people, I have to accept the mess that life often is and get on with it. What a relief that tidiness is not a fruit of the Spirit.

Sunday, 24 November

I returned our small visitor to his own home today and went in to see his dad in hospital. It was great to see him looking much better than I expected. He hopes to be home by Christmas. He wanted to hear all about the Lancashire option and thinks we should go for it. If only we could be so sure.

Monday, 25 November

I am away again, speaking for two days and staying at a conference centre in Derbyshire. David's potential new boss came to see him today and I got through at ten o'clock this evening to hear how the visit had gone. I could hear David's excitement down the phone line. I didn't really need to ask if he wanted the job. Nothing is settled yet, mind you; he'll have to go for an interview in January. I came back to my little room from the callbox and, looking for some undemanding reading to help me unwind, I flipped open the tourist information pack on the bedside cabinet. The first brochure on the pile had the words 'Welcome to Lancashire' written in large letters on the front. Everywhere I look I seem to be directed north.

Tuesday, 26 November

Our home group met this evening. Only two of them know about David's job offer. We have decided to limit the number of people we talk to because we don't want to risk the children hearing about unsettling possibilities before we tell them anything definite ourselves.

I enjoyed our evening together. I shall be very sad to leave these friends.

Sunday, 1 December

The social season gets under way and the calendar is covered with jottings and reminders. We are out three nights this week for practices for concerts and performances of different kinds. This is also the season for Scout bazaars and school Christmas fairs. I must find time to rummage through the children's rooms – there must be at least two bags of jumble I could shift.

This is also the disappearing season. At this time of year it is primarily money that disappears at an alarming rate, but husbands are also known to disappear on suspiciously solitary shopping trips, and as for the handy Sellotape dispenser that's meant to sit on my desk . . .

A disappearance of another sort is bothering me at the moment. Last Monday evening I recall seeing my slippers in the hallway, near the bottom of the stairs, a fairly popular location for discarded footwear of any kind. This was the last recorded sighting of them.

By Tuesday I was vaguely aware of their absence and by teatime the cold kitchen floor underfoot prompted a search. David generously offered extra pocket money to anyone who found Mum's slippers and this motivated the children to a full half-hour search. They looked behind sofas, under beds, in cupboards, even in the laundry basket, all to no avail.

By Wednesday I was wearing two pairs of socks and harbouring malicious feelings towards the dog. But he couldn't have stolen and buried both slippers, surely? They were big boot slippers, not your dainty ballerina types. You'd have thought they'd be difficult to lose.

On Thursday, having conducted my own search of the premises, I went into town to buy more slippers. I was sure this activity in itself would smoke out the original pair. How often have I found a missing item shortly after replacing it? I bought a conspicuously bright pair of cheap and nasties, which I now have to live with because my old slippers have not succumbed to my psychological manoeuvrings.

This evening another possibility as to their whereabouts occurred to me. Maybe my son, finding himself not up to the economic challenge of Christmas presents, has purloined them. Even now they could be lying, wrapped up, at the back of some cupboard, waiting to be rediscovered on Christmas Day, in which case I suppose I shall have to feign delight.

I probably shouldn't accuse him of such deviousness, but comfort deprivation can sour the mind.

Wednesday, 4 December

Still no sign of the slippers, but I've stopped accusing the dog. He can't even hide his bone with any great success, let alone two size 5 slippers. He has very strong digging instinct, which isn't very helpful as he spends most of his time indoors. He has to make do with burying his bone wherever he can: under newspapers, loose carpets, sofa cushions . . . What he really wants is to dig a pit for it in the garden, but as I don't let him out to do so, he wanders round the house with it, whimpering pitifully.

So far this seems to be his only complex, so I think we'll forgive him. I'm finding dog-ownership surprisingly therapeutic. There's nothing like getting up at dawn to stand in the back garden in my dressing gown, murmuring words of encouragement and doing the same again last thing at night. All this fresh air must be good for me. I also go out to the garden with him every two hours and take him for at least two walks a day. This is all meant to be for his benefit, not mine, but I'm getting to like the routine. It's nice to have an excuse to sit down and do very little, except pat a puppy, several times a day. And while I work, my little companion sits at my feet and rewards me with affection bordering on adoration (I can take it).

Friday, 6 December

David has been away again for part of this week. I don't think the new job will offer any let-up in the amount he has to travel. Our decision has been on my mind a lot this week. I was reading in Isaiah 7 about the sign given to the people of Israel: 'The virgin will be with child and will give birth to a son . . .' It made me wonder if it would be right for us to ask for a sign. I didn't have anything quite so dramatic in mind, and I'd prefer not to wait nine months for it.

To move such a long way north, away from our friends, further from our families, uprooting the children, giving up everything that I enjoy doing here . . . it seems such a bizarre thing to ask us to do. I wonder if, in fact, God has asked us? Is this job offer just a distraction and not a new direction at all? If it is a new direction, I'm going to have a really hard time saying 'yes' to it.

A sign pointing us in the right direction would be helpful, but I don't know if it's right to ask for a sign. After all, 'Do not put the Lord your God to the test.' It hardly seems like an expression of trust, but then again I'm only asking for reassurance, and I wouldn't hesitate to reassure my children if they were feeling hesitant about something. The other problem with a sign is that I don't know what to ask for. I know Gideon put out his fleece to catch and then not catch the dew, but I don't think the children would be very impressed if I tried the same with theirs. Anyway I've always thought Gideon was a bit of a wimp, asking for reassurance at every turn, even if God didn't seem to mind. The trouble is that if I don't specify exactly what sign I'd like, how will I know it when I see it? How will I be sure I'm not conning myself?

This guidance business is very tricky. I've decided not to ask for a sign, but I have asked if it's okay to ask for a sign and I haven't had an answer . . . yet.

Sunday, 8 December

I'd forgotten about Friday's dithering over signs when I went to church this morning, but at the end of the service, when the words of encouragement to come for prayer ministry were given out, I was suddenly all ears. 'Call to me and I will answer you and tell you great and unsearchable things you do not know [Jeremiah 33:3],' read the service leader and followed it up with the hint that this was for someone struggling with a difficult decision. He might as well have called me out by name. Here was my permission to ask for a sign.

I didn't tell the prayer team what the decision was about. We just prayed that I'd know the right thing to do. Nothing else happened, no flashing lights or warm glow, no certainty about whether we should stay or go, just relief at having prayed about it and a sense of peace that the matter had been handed over to God.

Emma also had a moment of triumph this morning in church. She was in Sunday school and her group were lagging behind in a team competition. At the last moment she single-handedly hauled them from the brink of undignified defeat by reciting the names of all sixty-six books of the Bible from memory and claiming the fifty bonus points on offer for such a feat. She has been secretly swotting for this opportunity, as she has always loved memorising things. My only hope is that she moves on to memorise more than the contents page.

Disconsolate over Sunday lunch, Matthew exclaimed that he only knew three books of the Bible: 1 Kings, 2 Kings and 'Generous'. I make that two books and one character trait – a timely one, given the time of year.

Monday, 9 December

I've found my slippers – oh, joy! They were stuffed down the back of a radiator.

Wednesday, 11 December

This morning before I opened my Bible I reminded

God about Sunday's request for a sign about whether or not we should move to Lancashire. I have been reading Zechariah, so I didn't hold out much hope of a sign from the passage before me (no disrespect to the Minor Prophets, but one has to admit that most of the 'Thus says the Lord' remarks are directed to the remnant of Israel, not to confused twentieth-century housewives). But I was in for a surprise. There in Zechariah, chapter six, verse eight, is one of the only references in the entire Bible to moving north, and it sounded positive to me. I laughed out loud and didn't really know what to make of it. I was brought up on careful Bible reading and know all about how dangerous it is to take one verse out of context, so I don't think I should make too much of this coincidence. Then again, I did ask for a sign. Maybe I'm just hard to please.

Sunday, 15 December

This morning at church I picked up a letter from a friend. I didn't open it until I got home. Her note was to thank me for something simple I'd done, but she had enclosed a poem that was meaningful to her. Aware that she knew nothing of our dilemma nor of my request for a sign, I sat down before I opened the folded poem.

'Help me to say yes' was the title. The opening line was I'm afraid of saying yes, Lord' and it went on for a whole page, poetically describing my exact feelings of loss at the thought of moving away:

> Where will you take me?
> I'm afraid of drawing the longer straw,
> I'm afraid of signing my name to
> an unread agreement . . .

As I turned the page God replied to the poet's fears:

> I want you to say yes . . .
> I need your yes to be united
> with you and come down to earth,
> I need your yes to continue saving the world.

I think I've had my answer. Now I just have to get used to the idea.

Monday, 16 December – of school Christmas concerts

Both kids came home from school today singing. It's not the end of term already; they've just been in rehearsals all day for tomorrow's school concert. If Emma hasn't been humming 'Little donkey', she's been singing 'Hey, little bull behind the gate'. As far as I can make out from the snippets I've heard so far, this year's production seems to be a straightforward nativity, perhaps slightly tipped in favour of the farm animals.

You can't always rely on a school Christmas concert to have anything to do with the Christmas story. A few years ago I went to see my goddaughter play the part of an elephant in an adaptation of a Rudyard Kipling tale. In the same concert I seem to recall small children dressed up as dice, but for the life of me I cannot remember the reason for this. At any rate, it was a concert devoid of Christian content.

We had a traditional nativity play last year, so if we're served up with another tomorrow, it will be a bonus. Last year Emma took the part of Mary, so I had to practise my 'modest mother of the child star' pose and we sat through every performance with lumps in our throats. For the most part she managed to look like a very demure Mary and only hissed once at some poor shepherds who inadvertently strayed in front of her. She couldn't help it. The disguise slipped and her true vocation of stage manager took over.

This year Matthew has been telling me the Christmas story in daily episodes as he receives it from Miss Watters. He tells it to me as if I've never heard it before, which is very refreshing. As any child in reception can tell you, the story concerns a certain Mary and Joe Fizz from Nas R F who travel on a very important donkey to a place called Befleahem in order to have a baby called Jesus. At least he's grasped the central event. Thank goodness she left Quirinius out of it!

All this solid Bible teaching is very reassuring,

given the mood in the high street. I haven't even thought about the Christmas shopping yet, but on Saturday I passed a large department store which had lavish displays in every window along with a slogan saying 'Debenhams – the gift of Christmas'. And there's me thinking that Jesus was the gift of Christmas. It's hard enough persuading them that Christmas isn't just about presents, chocolate, too much TV and yet more chocolate. I can do without that kind of propaganda.

Wednesday, 18 December – more of Christmas concerts

The concert: I went along this evening to the first sitting on the second day of performances. David is full of a cold and feeling miserable so he had to miss it this year, which is a shame, especially as he missed a real treat. It was a nativity play with lots of songs, angels and at least three animals. It finished with the lights going down as two children from the reception class sang a duet together. This had you reaching for your hanky but, just to surprise you, as they finished strings of party lights suddenly came on around the room and the whole school joined in at full volume with the chorus, 'Now light one thousand Christmas lights'. Very effective. Full marks for impact.

I love school Christmas concerts. The one thing you can always guarantee is the large turn-out.

This year the children had to do the whole thing three times so that everyone could get to see it. Grannies and aunties compete for spare seats. Video cameras roll and flash bulbs explode as every little starlet comes forward to say their lines. Mummies mouth the well-rehearsed lines to encourage their offspring. Grandads lean forward to catch every word. It's just about the most undivided attention any child could want.

Of course, for some it goes to their heads. I heard the story of one little boy who had to play the part of an innkeeper who said, 'No room,' when he really wanted to be the innkeeper with the stable. He brought the whole plot to a standstill when he threw open his inn door and said, 'Yes, I've got room. Come on in.'

The most memorable nativity play I've ever seen was the one at Emma's nursery school. It was a mixed nursery which took some able-bodied children as well as some with special needs. Mary and Joseph were played by two children with Down's syndrome who beamed at the audience throughout the whole performance and were so pleased with themselves that they hugged each other regularly. Heart-warming wasn't the word for it.

I like to think that whenever I offer up my performance to God, whether it's preparing something, speaking somewhere or simply being a mum, he leans forward like a parent at a nativity play, smiling encouragement, keen to catch my every word, looking for every nuance in my face. I don't imagine him sitting back with his arms folded, like some hard-to-please critic, which is just as well because not all my performances are good ones.

The ghost of Christmas Past comes back to haunt me. Last year's Children's Crib Service on Christmas Eve was nearly a disaster and it was all my fault. It wouldn't have mattered so much but my oversight seemed to sum up my spiritual condition at the time. I suppose now is as good a time as any to exorcise the ghost.

A year ago in November the Mother and Toddler Group committee met to plan the Christmas Eve Crib Service. What had begun a few years before as a very simple 'turn up and take part' nativity play for toddlers had grown into one of the key services over the Christmas season.

We wondered how we could make this year's offering fresh and original. As the conversation ranged around the seasonal trappings of turkey and tinsel, someone came up with an idea for the theme: 'Don't leave Jesus out of Christmas.' This reminded someone else of an excellent sketch on that very theme and the service began to take shape.

We decided to stick with the tradition of 'turn up and take part'. This means that on the day we have upwards of twenty kings and thirty shepherds, all under five. They arrive, dressed by their mummies and ready for action. (Shepherd outfits come more easily to hand, hence the imbalance.)

The performance consists of long pieces of music during which all the costumed tiny tots parade around the church and someone narrates the story. The key players in the story have been chosen from among the older children, and are already in place at the front. After some time spent milling about, the shepherds and kings finally wend their way on stage to form a sort of tableau around the little family.

This year we decided to invite the little girls to come as angels. This was a popular decision. We were visited by a host of small heavenly beings with coat-hanger haloes and bent-wire wings. As my own little girl was playing Mary at school, she didn't get a big part in the church production, but her stardom did give me the courage to ask if we could borrow the school's nativity outfits. Generously, they agreed.

This meant I only had Matthew to dress as a shepherd, as well as remember the tape of music, wrap up three cans in foil for the gifts, take the shepherd's crook, spare tabards for any undressed latecomers and my notes for the three-minute talk I was to give after the play and learn my lines for the drama. (Well, it's not as if you have anything else to think about on Christmas Eve, is it?)

The service was at 5 p.m. All afternoon I had this nagging feeling that I'd forgotten something, but I just couldn't find a few moments to think it over. We arrived in good time and all the key players turned up and dressed up in the school costumes.

Just before five, the shepherds and kings arrived in their droves and the service looked set to be a success.

The nativity play was the crowd-puller but we hoped the drama would hit home. It was to follow on immediately after the end of the play. John, our curate, was to come down the aisle pretending to be a photographer and ask if he could take a picture for our local paper. (He had heard there was this great story about a mother and baby in stable condition.)

After much jostling he was meant to declare that the only way to fit all the children into the picture would be to get rid of that rather grubby-looking manger. Having done so, he'd then take his picture but, of course, miss the whole point of the story.

Only as the final few shepherds were squeezing their way on to the stage did it suddenly dawn on me what was missing. I'd forgotten Jesus and the manger. There was Mary, there was Joseph, but no baby and no manger. How on earth could I have forgotten them? I was supposed to have brought them and the whole drama hinged on their presence.

Crouched behind the front pew, I wanted the ground to open up and swallow me. The 'photographer' was about to make his entrance. I needed a baby Jesus in a crib and I needed him fast. Explaining the imminent disaster to a friend behind me, she offered me her guitar case and I considered it for a

'It's hard to make a convincing baby out of tea towels....'

moment. Bethlehem's baby laid in a guitar case: I didn't think we'd get away with it.

The kitchenette in the side aisle was my only hope. I scuttled across the scene, dived into a cupboard, pulled out a box, threw flower-arranging equipment in all directions and stuffed it with tea towels. It's hard to make a convincing baby out of tea towels in under ten seconds, but I tried.

Telling myself how stupid I was and forgetting my radio mike was switched on, I crawled back to the stage and just managed to shove the box at Mary's feet before standing up to deliver the first line in the drama. Unaware of my panic, John played out his role with conviction. Several parents thought he was a genuine photographer and asked for the picture afterwards.

My heart rate had hardly recovered before it was time for the talk. Somewhere in the crisis I'd lost my notes, so I had to ad lib it. Red-faced and blatantly hypocritical, I delivered with conviction the only line I could remember. 'Don't leave Jesus out of Christmas,' I declared, adding under my breath, 'like I just have.'

This year, whatever else goes wrong, I will not forget to take Jesus with me – not a bad motto for any occasion.

Saturday, 21 December

The last Saturday before Christmas is not a good

day for buying your husband's Christmas present, especially when you've no idea what to get him. It would have helped to remember what I gave him last year. The range of things that interest him is so limited that I run a high risk of getting him the same thing two years running. He refuses clothes (unless they are from his mother), likes computer games (too pricey) and food (too cheap). His criteria for a good present is that it should be large, heavy and useful. I have only once found anything that qualified – a wooden toilet seat – and he was delighted with it.

Today I struggled around town for about two hours, trying to decide on something. Then I had a brainwave: a rechargeable torch. He has a torch, but the children constantly borrow it for their den in the under the stairs cupboard and leave it on. Whenever we need it the batteries are flat. I found just the thing at just the right price, so it was a good morning's work after all. I hope he likes it.

Monday, 23 December

David's holiday started today and we got off to a good start by taking the children to a pantomine. There was plenty of 'Oh, no he isn't,' 'He's behind you,' etc., as well as the ritual humiliation of unwilling volunteers. The kids loved it. I suppose it makes a good Christmas memory to store away, but once you've seen one pantomine, you've seen them all.

The Christmas memories I treasure are of Emma singing a solo of 'Away in a manger', standing on a chair at the back of Gran's church, and Matthew's face when he first heard the little train in his junior train set go 'Toot! Toot!' as it went over the hill. That 'Toot!Toot!' drove me nutty for the following three months, but he adored it.

This year we hope his eyes will light up when he sees the bike we have for him, currently hiding away in our neighbour's shed. Emma is having a stationery Christmas. I think this will please the administrator in her. Emma was born to organise.

Not all my memories are good ones. The Christmas when I was expecting Emma was the Christmas that wasn't a Christmas at all. Dad had a heart attack on the 21st of December and never recovered consciousness before he died on the 27th. I think we went through the motions of Christmas for the sake of the grandchildren, but my lasting memory from that year was the sense of close support within the family and an acute awareness of God. This year I seem to have missed him more than ever, but that's probably because of all the uncertainty surrounding the job in Lancashire. David's father died just six weeks after mine, also quite unexpectedly. Suddenly we became the older generation. Previously used to having fathers on hand for advice, the situation reversed itself as both widowed mums bravely learnt to live alone. At times like this, I miss an earthly father. I know

I have a heavenly one but sometimes . . . Oh, well, it doesn't do to get morose, especially at this time of year.

Christmas Eve

The Crib Service went brilliantly. I have shaken off the effect of last year's near disaster. The children enjoyed themselves, the balloons descended from the balcony on time and all the little performers went home with a candy stick for their tree.

Then this evening, of all evenings, Emma cornered me at bed-time. 'I want to know the whole truth about Father Christmas,' she said in a very determined tone. I was tempted to fudge the issue but I don't like to lie outright and she clearly wasn't going to take any waffle, so I told her. Father Christmas has never had that big a part to play in our celebrations anyway. He only brings the cheap presents at the end of your bed, whereas Mummy and Daddy give proper ones under the tree (why should he get the credit for our hard-earned generosity?).

She didn't seem that shocked when I told her. I think she'd already guessed. Her letter to Santa was a bit of a give-away: assuming he shopped in our town, she'd written it complete with the names of the shops where her heart's desires could be purchased.

She didn't breathe a word to Matthew and went off to bed quite content.

Christmas Day

Last night's revelations didn't dampen Emma's enthusiasm for her Christmas stocking. She entered into the game with just as much vigour as ever.

I caught the tail-end of the Queen's speech on the radio as I prepared the meal. It brought a lump to my throat, even though I'm not a very patriotic royalist. It was what she said about not looking back and saying, 'If only . . .' but looking forward and saying, 'If only we can imitate Jesus, then we can go forward without fear and in faith.' I felt she was speaking just to me.

The day has panned out very well. I felt a bit nostalgic and tearful at the start, but Her Majesty helped to pull me out of this mood. The children have been delighted with all their gifts, David was very pleased with his torch and I have been overwhelmed with bubble bath. I have obviously reached that stage in life when I'll never be a bridesmaid again, my children describe me as old and everyone gives me bubble bath for Christmas. Just as well I like the stuff.

Tomorrow Gran comes to stay and we do it all over again except this time with a turkey. Today the children had toad-in-the hole for their Christmas lunch because it's their favourite and David and

I had steak. It made the day much more relaxing.

Saturday, 28 December

We've had a great time with Gran. Her gift to Matthew has gone down particularly well: a talking, zapping Buzz Lightyear, that well-known intergalatic space traveller. Although he hadn't specifically asked for one, he tore off the paper and exclaimed, 'I really wanted one of these!' bang on cue, much to the satisfaction of Gran, who had provided it, and his mum who had suggested it.

Matthew and Buzz have had a great time playing together. There have already been moments when David and I felt that if we heard him say, 'To infinity and beyond!' one more time, then that is where he would be sent. His chirpy chat-up line wears thin after a while, but the batteries can't last for ever.

Tuesday, 31 December

I've been dipping into Oswald Chambers's *My Utmost for His Highest* again. I seem to remember reading it this time last year and learning that it was okay to feel empty and spiritually dried up. The bit I read today was particularly helpful regarding our uncertain future, although I suppose I shouldn't call it uncertain now that I've had my sign. It went as follows, with my response in brackets: 'Have you been asking God what he is going to do?' (Yes, repeatedly.) 'He will never tell you.' (Bother.) 'God does not tell you what he is going to do – he reveals to you who he is.' (Hmm.)

It's a sad fact that I'm still much more interested in what's about to happen in my little life than in discovering deeper shades and hues in my understanding of God as my Father. I guess I've still got a long way to go. I feel like I've travelled quite a distance in this year's journey. When I look back on how dispirited I was feeling this time last year I realise I've come a long way. I may feel uncertain but I do at least believe that God is holding the maps and knows where he is taking me.

Of course, progress hasn't been in a straight line, but when is it ever? There was the excitement of trying to move and the disappointment when we couldn't (just as well we didn't, though, isn't it?). Then there was all the uncertainty about whether or not to extend, which finally resolved itself and resulted in the house being rearranged while we were away on holiday. That wasn't an easy holiday. I never want to go anywhere wet and green again. Give me dry, hot and brown every time.

And now ahead of us there is the possibility of a move to Lancashire and starting all over again with a new home, new church, new friends. When I first began to pray about this move one of the things God reminded me of was that no home is permanent and the whole of life is merely a journey between this world and the next. Somewhere in a hymn there is the line 'We nightly pitch our tent a day's march nearer home.' I grew up listening to Jim Reeves, my father's favourite, so I've known from infancy that 'This world is not my home. I'm just a-passing through. /My treasures are laid up somewhere beyond the blue.'

The main difficulty about journeys is that you don't know where to set your sights. For most of the last month my sights have been fixed too far ahead: where will we live, where will we worship, etc. I have wasted the now, the today, I've been given because I have been too preoccupied with tomorrow. What was it Jesus said? '. . . do not worry about tomorrow, for tomorrow will worry about itself.' Easier said than done. I've also started to grieve for the many good friends we'll leave behind, and I sense God loosening my ties. It's hard to be a pilgrim when your security is too strongly attached to where you live or who you are near.

I'm impatient to know when and how it's all going to happen. I don't like living in the limbo of uncertainty. I am like a small child on the back seat of a car half an hour into a long journey, asking, 'Are we nearly there yet?' every five minutes. I've very little idea of where 'there' is, but at least I know who is in the driving seat.

The children, of course, still don't know anything about the impending move. This evening I asked them about their hopes for the New Year. What did they think the future held?

'I don't know what the word "future" means,' Matthew said cheerfully. He understands 'tomorrow' and 'on Saturday' and maybe even 'end of term' but 'future' is a concept too vast for him to take in and he seems quite happy to leave it that way.

'Become like a child,' said Jesus. Be safe in the knowledge of who your Father is and of how much he loves you, not in knowing each detail of everything he's planned for you. Clearly, in spite of my resolution last New Year's Day, I still have a lot to learn from my children.

The other night I had a dream. I dreamt I was holding a very long stethoscope up to God's heart. I was expecting to hear the 'bdum, bdum' noise that I remember from sitting with my head on my father's chest. I was listening for a sound that said, 'God is alive and well,' but the heartbeat of God was much more intimate than I expected. It said: 'I love you, I love you, I love you.' I woke amazed.

If that's the case, I thought to myself, *perhaps I can cope with limbo for just a bit longer.*

Epilogue

When you start a story in the middle, as I have with this diary, where do you stop? Life goes on; the story is always to be continued; every day is another turn in the road that leads us all the way home to heaven.

As I write we are in the process of moving to Lancashire. David got his job and God graciously gave us more reassurances about this new direction than we ought to have needed. The children, who were very upset at first, are now quite excited. Psalm 32:8–10 has become very meaningful to me:

> I will instruct you and teach you in the
> way you should go;
> I will counsel you and watch over you.
> Do not be like the horse or the mule, which
> have no understanding but must be controlled
> by bit and bridle or they will not come to you.
> Many are the woes of the wicked, but the
> LORD's unfailing love surrounds the man who
> trusts in him.

There are still many unanswered questions. Many aspects of the future seem uncertain, but if God has promised to be there when we arrive, then I think I can cope.

I hope that this inside view of the ups and downs

of a year in the life of our family encourages you in your family's journey. This could have been the story of any family with children: rows and arguments, pets and problems, parent evenings, holidays, money worries. This is the stuff of ordinary family life. I haven't written a diary about us because we are special in any way (although all of us are special to God) but because we are ordinary, and my prayer is that it will not only entertain you, but also help you to catch a glimpse of God and his love in the midst of your everyday life.

I'd like to thank my family, without whose permission this could not have been written. Their enthusiastic support has meant so much. Also thanks to the many friends who will find themselves in the pages of this book, although under different names. The strong threads of encouragement you provided really enriched the fabric of our lives. Thank you for allowing me to write about you.

Finally, my thanks to three people whose skilful editing has greatly enhanced this project: Jill Worth, Russ Bravo, for whom much of this material was originally prepared (and subsequently published in *Parentwise* and *New Christian Herald*), and Elspeth Taylor, who guided it into its final format.

THE ART OF IMPERFECT PARENTING

Sheila Bridge

An outrageously honest book that looks at the difficulties of being an effective parent.

Everyday real parents experience feelings of frustration, irritation and anxiety about their role. The fact that they know there must be a better way to bring up children doesn't help. This book, rather than being yet another 'how to get it right' book, is bold enough to recognise the feelings that all parents experience, and helps them to find hope when they know they've got it wrong.

Offering plenty of real-life, often humorous illustrations, it reveals how joy can be found in the midst of the hard work and hassle of family life.

ISBN 0 340 62134 6

THE ART OF PLATE SPINNING

Sheila Bridge

This book is for women who feel expected to juggle with motherhood, pursue a career, run church events, maintain their marriage and look good into the bargain.

As more and more women join the labour market, many feel that they no longer have the luxury of doing anything full-time. The sensation of being pulled simultaneously in several different directions can be bewildering. Sheila Bridge charts a way through the confusion of being a mother with a crowded lifestyle, and reveals how we can do all that we want to – without being overcome by exhaustion.

'*All the wonderful stages of motherhood would have been even more enjoyable if I had had this invaluable book to hand.*' Michele Guinness

ISBN 0 340 66185 2